DECODING
ANCIENT AMERICA

∽∽∽∽∽

A Guide to the Archaeology of
the Book of Mormon

DECODING
ANCIENT AMERICA

A Guide to the Archaeology of
the Book of Mormon

by DIANE E. WIRTH

HORIZON PUBLISHERS
SPRINGVILLE, UTAH

This is not an official publication of The Church of Jesus Christ of Latter-day Saints. The opinions and views expressed herein belong solely to the author and do not necessarily represent the opinions or views of Cedar Fort, Inc. Permission for the use of sources, graphics, and photos is also solely the responsibility of the author.

ISBN 13: 978-0-88290-820-5

Published by Horizon Publishers an imprint of Cedar Fort, Inc., 2373 W. 700 S., Springville, UT, 84663
Distributed by Cedar Fort, Inc., www.cedarfort.com

LIBRARY OF CONGRESS CATALOGING-IN-PUBLICATION DATA

    Wirth, Diane E.
    Decoding the ancient Americas : a guide to the archaeology of the book
    of Mormon / Diane E. Wirth.
       p. cm.
    ISBN-13: 978-0-88290-820-5
    1. Book of Mormon—Evidences, authority, etc. 2. Book of
    Mormon—Antiquities. 3. America—Antiquities. I. Title.
     BX8627.W67 2007
     289.3'22—dc22
                        2006039838

Cover design by Nicole Williams
Cover design © 2007 by Lyle Mortimer
Edited and typeset by Kammi Rencher

Printed in the United States of America

10 9 8 7 6 5 4 3 2 1

Printed on acid-free paper

DEDICATION

To the descendants of Lehi

ACKNOWLEDGMENTS

In order of their reading the manuscript, a special thank you to Allen Christenson, Cal Tolman, Garth Norman, John Tvedtnes, John Welch, Kevin Barney, and Jared Decker, who reviewed the text and offered valuable comments and insightful suggestions.

TABLE OF CONTENTS

To probe and ponder the circumstantial evidences of the scripture's truthfulness is one of the purposes of Book of Mormon research.

—John W. Welch

Introduction in *Reexploring the Book of Mormon*, ed. John W. Welch (Salt Lake City: Deseret Book; Provo: Foundation for Ancient Research and Mormon Studies, 1992)

A WORD ABOUT THIS BOOK

IN THE TEXT OF THIS BOOK, a number has been assigned to many of the ideas expressed. If you want to read and learn more about a particular subject, you can find additional sources by referring to the corresponding number in the *List of Books and Sources* at the back of the book.

Some of the illustrations in this book are drawings from ancient books called *codices* (one book is a codex). These ancient books and most of the drawings in this book were made many hundreds of years after the close of the Book of Mormon but before the Spanish troops of Cortez arrived in AD 1519. This event is called the Spanish Conquest. A few of these old books were illustrated after the Spanish came to Mexico and Central America. Therefore, illustrations with a picture from a codex will state either *Pre-Conquest*, before the Spanish arrived, or *Early Post-Conquest*, soon after the Spanish arrived.

As you will notice, most pictures have a number. For those who are interested, locate the numbers in the *List of Books and Sources* in the back of this book to find where you can see these pictures to learn more. However, some pictures from the codices are rather hard to locate, unless your library has a copy of the codex. Many pictures from codices are published in other books, which are also listed in the *List of Books and Sources*.

CHAPTER ONE

༺ⓔⓔⓔⓔⓔ༻

The location of the lands of the Book of Mormon

THE SCRIPTURES INDICATE that the lands of the Book of Mormon comprised three major areas: the land northward, the land southward, and the narrow neck of land. This could be North and South America, with Panama as the narrow neck of land, or it could be the smaller area of Mexico and Central America, with the Isthmus of Tehuantepec as the narrow neck of land. Many of the early Church leaders thought that the Book of Mormon took place in North and South America. However, there are many clues that the lands where the Book of Mormon people lived comprised a much smaller area, encompassing only parts of Mexico and Central America.

The more limited location described above is the opinion of most Latter-day Saint archaeologists, those dedicated people who piece together the puzzles of the past by going through the remains that ancient people left in their lands, their buildings, and their works of art. Mesoamerica is the land that archaeologists define as ancient Mexico and Central America.

The small box in Figure 1 shows the area known as Mesoamerica within the Americas. It is between Central Mexico and just before Costa Rica and Panama in South America. The countries of Central America that will be mentioned in this book are Guatemala, Belize, Honduras, and El Salvador. The states in Mexico that are mentioned are Puebla, Morelos, Veracruz, Tabasco, Campeche, Chiapas, and Yucatan.

Figure 1.
Map of the
Americas.

For clarification, we will use the word *Mexican* to refer to those ancient tribes that lived in the country we call Mexico. The name *Mexico* was derived from the Mexica tribe, one of seven Aztec tribal groups that lived in this area anciently. However, it is also important to realize that there were many other ancient tribes that lived within the Mexican proper, such as the Zapotec, Mixtec, Toltec, Huastec, Teotihuacano, and Mezcala, to name a few.

The Lord has never revealed where the Book of Mormon history took place. However, Joseph Smith, the first LDS Church prophet and the editor of the Church's newspaper, *Times and Seasons*, stated that the city of Zarahemla, which burned at the time of the crucifixion of the Savior, was in Guatemala.[1]

In Joseph Smith's day, Guatemala was larger than it is today, and we know from the scriptures that Zarahemla was in the land southward (see Mormon 1:6). That would mean that the land northward was roughly what is now Mexico, and the Isthmus of

Tehuantepec would have been the narrow neck of land (see Alma 63:5). This is just one of the clues that point to Mesoamerica as the lands of the Book of Mormon.

If we use Joseph Smith's basic model of Mesoamerica, we can visualize the general location of the lands mentioned in the Book of Mormon (see Fig. 2). Figure 3 shows the major cultures that lived in Mesoamerica. It is crucial to remember that the Book of Mormon

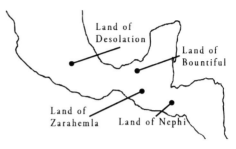

Figure 2. Proposed Book of Mormon lands in Mesoamerica.

contains only limited history and geography; its primary purpose is to be another testament of Jesus Christ, containing the gospel message of the prophets to their people and the teachings of our Savior.

Many scholars have attempted to pinpoint the exact location of Nephite cities within Mesoamerica. However, this may not be possible unless evidence is found at a site that can be identified as a city in the Book of Mormon. Actually, many Book of Mormon cities may have been discovered, but they are now called different names than they are labeled in the scriptures. Therefore, LDS archaeologists cannot be specific, because the names of these cities have been changed since the time of the Book of Mormon.

Figure 3. Cultures in Mesoamerica.

So how can we connect this area to the lands of the Book of Mormon? There are actually several similarities between the lands of the Book of Mormon and Mesoamerica that point to Mesoamerica as the location of the Book of Mormon peoples. To name a few: buildings made with cement, roads that connect cities, walled cities with fortifications for protection, the prevalence of fevers during certain seasons of the year, and a number of advanced writing systems. All of the above are mentioned in the Book of Mormon and are obvious in Mesoamerica but are not predominant in North and South America.

Ancient North and South American people did not build with cement. Both North and South America had roads anciently but not to the extent that they existed in Mesoamerica; the same is true of fortifications. Fevers were not prevalent in North and South America due to the nature of the climates. South America had no ancient writing system during Book of Mormon times, and most writings found by nonprofessional archaeologists in North America have yet to be proven as authentic. Let us go through these items and explain their significance in uniting the Book of Mormon lands with Mesoamerica.

CEMENT

> And there being but little timber upon the face of the land, nevertheless the people who went forth became exceedingly expert in the working of cement; therefore they did build houses of cement, in the which they did dwell. (Helaman 3:7).

When the Nephites traveled to the lands northward, they built with cement as they had done in the land southward. Many of the buildings in Mesoamerica were covered with a type of stucco, which may be termed *cement*. In this way, they were able to mold designs as they wished. Murals were painted on stucco, and in fact, most building exteriors were brightly painted with red, blue, green, and yellow on a surface of stucco. The making of cement or stucco is a difficult process that takes skilled craftsmanship. Actually, it takes a great deal of limestone and an even greater amount of wood to create a few cups of stucco/cement. Today visitors will notice a scarcity of wood. Scholars agree that in parts of Mesoamerica the forests were largely destroyed by AD 100 due to the making of stucco. Since wood was scarce, the Nephites had timber shipped in from other locales (see Helaman 3:10).

ROADS

And there were many highways cast up, and many roads made, which led from city to city, and from land to land, and from place to place (3 Nephi 6:8).

Imagine great highways linking the cities of the Nephites and perhaps those of the Lamanites. Roads connected cities throughout Mesoamerica and were raised up from the ground with stone, oftentimes overlaid with cement. The Book of Mormon refers to roads being "cast up," and that is exactly how they built their raised highways. Archaeologists call these roads causeways. These causeways connected one city to another, spreading out like the spokes of a wheel from a central city. This was done during Book of Mormon times.

WALLED CITIES AND FORTIFICATIONS

Thus Moroni did prepare strongholds against the coming of their enemies, round about every city in all the land. (Alma 50:6)

Becan, in the Mexican state of Campeche, is probably the most well known city for walls and fortification (see Fig. 4). Almost every pre-Classic site dating between 400 BC and AD 250, which is right in the heart of Book of Mormon times, is known to have a fortification surrounding it.[2] These fortifications were necessary due to warfare throughout the land, as recorded in the Book of Mormon.

A ditch, or moat, in front of a wall was often one way to make a fortification against enemies in Mesoamerica. Today many of the walls can no longer be seen because the stones were used by later cultures for their buildings. There is evidence of this.

It is amazing that thirty years ago, the Maya in the eastern parts of Mexico and Central America were considered to have been a peaceful culture, unlike the warring cultures described in the Book of Mormon. Today we know that, in reality, the Mesoamericans were almost constantly at war. The Aztecs sacrificed many hundreds of their captives, and the Maya thought killing the kings of their enemies made them more powerful.[3] Building fortifications was necessary for survival.

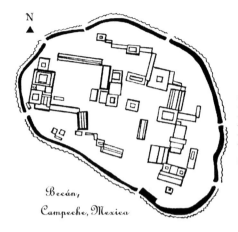

N

Figure 4. Fortification at
Becán, Campeche, Mexico.
Becán began about 600 BC
and declined by AD 1000.

Becán,
Campeche, Mexico

TROPICAL CLIMATE

And there were some who died with fevers, which at some seasons
of the year were very frequent in the land. (Alma 46:40)

The Book of Mormon lands in the eastern portion of
Mesoamerica had a tropical, hot climate, and sickness from fevers
was common. During one of their battles, Amalickiah and his
men were overpowered with fatigue because of the heat of the day.
Because of their fatigue, Teancum and his servant were able to put
a javelin to the heart of Amalickiah, thus causing the death of this
king (see Alma 51:33–34).

The Lamanites, in particular, often wore little clothing for battle
(see Alma 43:20). Even though it may have been uncomfortable, the
Nephites wore thick clothing for protection against their enemies
(see Alma 43:19). After the end of the Nephite culture, many people
of Mesoamerica adopted this padded-type clothing, which can now
be seen in sculptures of warriors (see Fig. 5).

WRITING SYSTEMS

And now there are many records kept of the proceedings of this
people, by many of this people, which are particular and very
large, concerning them. (Helaman 3:13)

We know from Mormon 9:32 that the Book of Mormon was
written in Reformed Egyptian, which consisted "of the learning of
the Jews and the language of the Egyptians" (1 Nephi 1:2).

Various Mexican cultures and the Maya to the east made picture books known as *codices* (singular codex). Codices have accordion-like pages that run many feet in length. To us today they appear to have a cartoon quality, primarily because most people do not understand what they mean. To the natives these codices told stories that those who were familiar with the legends of their forefathers could understand. Archaeologists can comprehend a portion of them.

Figure 5. Maya Warrior with protective clothing, from Jaina, Yucatan, Mexico.[4]

The most well known writing system in Mesoamerica is Maya (see Fig. 6).[5] Maya hieroglyphs differ from Egyptian hieroglyphs, but the individual glyphs were pronounced in a similar way; in other words, they both used a phonetic system to pronounce syllables. There is also an earlier system of writing in Mesoamerica called Epi-Olmec, which scholars are working on now. In either case, the hieroglyphs in Mesoamerica are not like the Book of Mormon script. We have a sample, known as the Anthon Transcript, that was copied from one of the golden plates. The Anthon Transcript shows us that Reformed Egyptian, the system used by Nephite writers, is very different from Maya hieroglyphs.

ti   *chan*

Figure 6. Maya Glyph *ti chan*, translated as "in heaven."

However, a few roller stamps (an object shaped like a small battery) have been found in Mesoamerica. Roller stamps were used by rolling the stamp on fabric or paper to get an impression of a design or written script. These stamps, often called cylinder seals, were also popular in the Near East, where the Lehites lived before they left their homeland for the promised land. One stamp in particular that was made in early Book of Mormon times, and found in Mexico, may be similar to the Nephite sampling from the Anthon Transcript (see Fig. 7).[6]

Figure 7. Roller stamp with inscription, from Tlatilco, Mexico.[6]

It must be remembered that the Nephites' system of writing was considered a unique and priestly script, not to be read by the common population. Those who wrote on the plates of the Book of Mormon had to be specifically schooled to do so. Even the Maya hieroglyphs could not be read by the common people. That is why Mesoamerican royalty used monumental art in order to communicate to their people an understanding of their religion, power, and politics.

LIMITED AREA

> And I [Moroni] even remain alone to write the sad tale of the destruction of my people. . . . Therefore I will write and hide up the records in the earth. (Mormon 8:3–4)

Moroni wrote the above scripture about AD 401, after the collapse of the Nephite nation through war, which happened approximately AD 385. Consequently, he had many years to travel and deposit the gold plates in a place of the Lord's choosing. Moroni did not mention a name for the hill in New York where he placed the plates in a stone box. However, many early Church members assumed this hill in New York was the same Hill Cumorah/Ramah where both the Nephites and the Jaredites fought their last battles.

We must also consider the travels and distances the people made as recorded in the Book of Mormon. Let us consider the Limhi expedition in Mosiah for an example (see Mosiah 8:7–11 and 21:25–27). This story may be the best argument against the Hill Cumorah in New York as being the same Hill Cumorah in the Book of Mormon.

In these verses in Mosiah, we read of a group of men who were headed from the land of Nephi to Zarahemla. Both locations were in the land southward, that is, south of the narrow neck of land (see Helaman 5:14, 16). Their grandparents had traveled from Zarahemla to Nephi and back two generations earlier (see Mosiah 7:9, 9:1–2).

For those who think that the Book of Mormon took place in both North America and South America, it is hard to believe that the Nephites traveled three thousand miles before they realized they missed Zarahemla. That would have been quite an oversight. They came to a place of bones from fallen Jaredite warriors. The men of the Lehi expedition also found the gold plates of Ether. Where was this? It was at Ramah, which is the same place that the Nephites called Cumorah (see Ether 15:11).

Limhi's men probably went through the narrow neck of land to the land northward in Mexico before they realized that they had missed Zarahemla. This was a trip of "many days" and a few hundred miles—not three thousand miles to what is now the state of New York.[7] (More discussion on the Hill Cumorah is contained in chapter 10 of this book.)

All these clues point to the theory that Mesoamerica is the land of the Book of Mormon. It is a limited area. The Book of Mormon describes these factors as being part of their history. However, in the nineteenth century when the Book of Mormon was translated by Joseph Smith, scholars scoffed at the idea of Native Americans having a high culture—people in those days thought the Native Americans were and always had been uncivilized. It was a general understanding that Indians did not have kings, could not write, did not make cement, and did not construct walls around their cities. With our awareness of archaeological discoveries since the Prophet's time, we now know otherwise.

As we continue with our quest for the best location of the Book of Mormon, we will look at other evidence that indicates Mesoamerica is the most likely place. Lehi and his party practiced many customs and beliefs in the Near East before they sailed to the "land of promise." We will examine some of these traditions to see if they can also be found in Mesoamerica.

Chapter Two

~~~~~~~

The people of the Book of Mormon

THE BOOK OF MORMON is a religious history of a people, namely the Nephites. We do not have a thorough account of the more numerous Lamanites, Mulekites, or any of the other groups that lived in the New World. In comparison, the Old Testament scriptures of the Bible also ignored other peoples' history. The histories of Egypt and Canaan are not mentioned in the Old Testament; only the history of Israel is recorded in the Bible. It was the same with most of the Book of Mormon. Nephite writers were concerned with gospel principles, their lineage, and history. The Book of Mormon history primarily focuses on the Nephite people who believed in Jesus Christ and those of their lineage who were less than righteous.

Were there Native American Indians already in the lands of the Book of Mormon when Lehi arrived? Most LDS archaeologists propose that there were people in America before Lehi's arrival.[8] The Jaredites arrived in the New World before Lehi's party, and the Mulekites came a few years after the Lehites. There may also have been others who made trips across the ocean. There is a particularly powerful scripture pointing to this conclusion. Lehi, speaking at the sunset of his life, prophesied about the land of promise when he said:

We have obtained a land of promise, a land which is choice above all other lands; a land which the Lord God hath covenanted with me should be a land for the inheritance of my seed. Yea, the Lord hath covenanted this land unto me, and to my children forever, *and also all those who should be led out of other countries* by the hand of the Lord. (2 Nephi 1:5; emphasis added)

THE JAREDITES

The earliest civilization accounted for in the Book of Mormon is that of the Jaredites. There is good reason to presume that there still may have been Jaredites in the land after the Jaredite nation fell.[9] They came to the Americas at the time of the Tower of Babel in Mesopotamia (Iraq today). Except for the language of the people of Jared, the languages of the land became confused. Jared's party was blessed with keeping their language. Only a little is known about the Jaredites, with our limited knowledge coming from the book of Ether, one of the last books in the Book of Mormon. However, we do know that they eventually became a wicked people.

The Jaredite nation was destroyed through a very bloody civil war. Most likely, not all of the people were killed. Remember the story of how Limhi's people discovered the Jaredites' twenty-four plates of gold when they became lost looking for Zarahemla? (See Mosiah 8.) Limhi wondered if Ammon could translate these inscribed plates because he was curious about the history of the Jaredite people. Referring to the Jaredites, Mosiah 8:12 mentions a "remnant of the people who have been destroyed." If there was a "remnant," there were people besides Coriantumr, the last Jaredite king, who survived the war.

Consider the Jaredite names such as Shiblon (Ether 1:12), Morianton (Ether 1:22–23), Nehor (Ether 7:9), and Corihor (Ether 7:3) being used among the Nephite people many years later (*Shiblon*, Mormon 6:14; *Morianton*, Alma 50:28; *Nehor*, Alma 1; and *Korihor*, Alma 30–31). Perhaps the use of Jaredite names continued because some Jaredites survived their great battle, and their descendants continued to use the names.

This points to evidence that not all of the Jaredites were destroyed in their last battle in Mesoamerica. In fact, many years later in the Maya city of Palenque, Chiapas, Mexico, an Olmec king named U-K'ix-Chan is mentioned. In the Mayan language, x is pronounced "sh." Therefore, K'ix would be pronounced "Kish," and Kish is a Jaredite name (see Ether 10: 17–18).[10] The Olmec were most likely what we call the Jaredites, because the Olmec nation lived and died about the same time in Mesoamerica. Again, this refers to their nation, not all the people.

A word about the Olmec civilization is needed here. It has long been considered by archaeologists that the Olmec were the "mother culture" of Mesoamerica. They lived primarily along the Gulf of Mexico to just a little east of the Isthmus of Tehuantepec (see Fig. 3). West of the Isthmus of Tehuantepec (the narrow neck of land) would be considered the land northward in the scriptures. This area was the Olmec heartland, although their influence has also been found elsewhere in Mesoamerica. So, we can readily see a correspondence of the Jaredite nation with the Olmec civilization.

THE MULEKITES

The name "Mulekite" is not mentioned in the Book of Mormon but was coined by LDS scholars because these people who were later called Mulekites descended from a son of King Zedekiah in Jerusalem who was brought to the Americas to avoid being taken captive into Babylon. King Zedekiah, the last king of Judah, was carried away into Babylon (see Omni 1:15; 2 Kings 25:7). The story of his surviving son, Mulek, is known only in the Book of Mormon. Mulek and his rescuers were brought across the great waters to the land of promise, into the land northward, by the Lord (see Helaman 6:10; Omni 1:15). The Mulekites, as we call them, were known to the Nephites as the people of Zarahemla, which was in the land southward (see Omni 1:13). The Nephites were also in the land southward, but they were located south of Zarahemla.

How did Mulek get to the new land across the sea? Many people who study the Book of Mormon propose the Phoenicians may have been instrumental in saving young Mulek and his party. It was the Phoenicians who helped build Solomon's temple for the Israelites. They were also known to have the best sailing ships of their time. The Phoenicians hired crews from all over the Near East. The crew would have been made up of many races of men with many different cultural traditions.

Something unique happened between the Mulekites and a king of the Jaredite people named Coriantumr (see Omni 1:21–22). Coriantumr was a ruler and a warrior. He witnessed the defeat of his nation through war. The Nephites heard about Coriantumr when they came to Zarahemla, which was a Mulekite city. There is an interesting stela (a sculpted rock monument) from La Venta, Mexico, made by the Olmec. John Sorenson, an LDS archaeologist, suggests that this stela may show a Jaredite on the left and a bearded Mulekite on the right (see Fig. 8).[8]

This stela is not small; it weighs fifty tons. On the left, we see a man with a short nose, wearing a cape and a loincloth. To

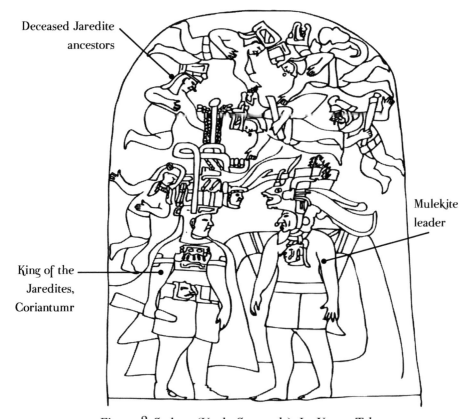

Deceased Jaredite ancestors

Mulekite leader

King of the Jaredites, Coriantumr

Figure 8. Stela 3 (Uncle Sam stela), La Venta, Tabasco, Mexico, about 600 BC.[11]

the right is a bearded man. How unusual! Native Indians of the Americas do not typically grow large beards. The archaeologists who found this stela nicknamed it "The Uncle Sam Stela," because the person to the right looks like Uncle Sam, who has a beard and a large hooked nose. (A note for the younger reader: Uncle Sam not only collects your taxes, but he is the person recruiting on posters for the U.S. armed services. He is dressed in red, white, and blue, and pointing his finger, he says, "I Want You.") In fact, the man on this stone carving found in Mexico looks like a Middle Easterner.[8] These two men, of different races, appear to be greeting each other.

Note the floating figures above these two men. Floating persons in Mesoamerican art often represent deceased ancestors. Could this be Coriantumr describing to a bearded Mulekite the story of their wars and the conclusion of the Jaredite nation? Do the floating people represent the thousands of Coriantumr's Jaredite warriors who died in their last battle?

Bearded Foreigners

Figure 8 is not the only Mesoamerican sculpture of a man with a beard; there are hundreds of them (see Fig. 9 for examples). But, if Indians can only grow a few hairs, which they plucked out, where did these bearded men come from? There is such diversity of people throughout Mesoamerica that the beards present quite the puzzle. Yet as we put the pieces together, it makes more sense, especially when we consider the Book of Mormon and where the people lived before in the Near East.

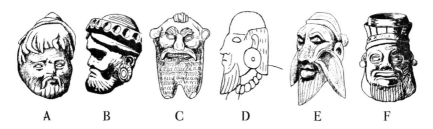

Figure 9. Bearded men from Mesoamerica. A, B, C, D, and E from Mexico; F from Guatamala. [12]

OTHER RACES

There apparently were many races in Mesoamerica (see Fig. 10). Letter E of Figure 10 is a typical Maya Indian. The others are of different races, yet they all dwelled in Mesoamerica. These portraits, made from clay or stone, were made for a special purpose. They meant something to the ancient people, the same as we have photographs of loved ones in our home or in our wallet. Each represented a particular person who once lived. Maybe some of these people were descendants of a crew on a Phoenician ship, or perhaps Asians traveling across the Bering Strait to the Americas.

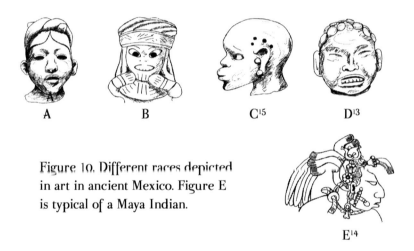

A   B   C[15]   D[13]

Figure 10. Different races depicted in art in ancient Mexico. Figure E is typical of a Maya Indian.

E[14]

THE SEVEN TRIBES

Nephi mentioned the first division of those that came with Lehi to the New World (see 2 Nephi 5:6). This division was recorded again in 543 BC.

> Now the people which were not Lamanites were Nephites; nevertheless, they were called Nephites, Jacobites, Josephites, Zoramites, Lamanites, Lemuelites, and Ishmaelites. (Jacob 1:13)

The first three, the Nephites, Jacobites, and Josephites, were considered Nephites. The last three, the Lamanites, Lemuelites, and Ishmaelites, were the Lamanites. Zoram was loyal to Nephi, but his descendants eventually changed their allegiance and joined the Lamanites. Since their ancestor, Zoram, was the slave of Laban, we do not know his tribal lineage or his descendants. He may not have even been an Israelite.

Almost seven hundred years later, approximately AD 231 (see 4 Nephi 1:37–38), these tribal divisions were mentioned again, indicating the enduring nature of the seven tribes in the Book of Mormon. The tribes are last referred to in Mormon 1:8 about AD 322, which is not many years before the final battle (or destruction) of the Nephite nation. However, this was not the end of the seven tribes, and the tribes were not easily forgotten in the historical records of native Mesoamericans.

There is a great tradition in Mesoamerica of the people's ancestors originally coming from seven tribes. There are several examples of this tradition in art, but first we need to understand what caves mean to Mesoamericans, even today. Caves are damp and can give shelter, especially in the rain forests of Central America. Rain was also believed to come from caves in the mountains. These legends, as depicted in Mesoamerican art, show that seven tribes came from seven caves. These caves are considered to be like a mother's womb. A mother's womb is a protective enclosure and is also associated with water.

Sahagun, an early Spanish friar, stated that the Indians believed that these caves referred to a ship or ships that brought their seven ancestral tribes to this land.[16] Caves in Mesoamerica were closely associated with birth and were considered the place of emergence. There are many examples, but we are only going to look at two of

Figure 11. The seven tribes in *Codex Duran* (Early Post-Conquest, Mexico).[97]

these designs. The seven tribes in seven caves may be seen in the *Codex Duran* (see Fig. 11). These caves, each with people inside, are easy to see.

When you look at the next drawing, you have to stretch your imagination and see as the ancient people saw, not as we do today. Look at Figure 12. This design is called *Chicomoztoc* and refers to the seven caves. Each petal of the seven caved flower-like design represents a different tribe of people. Footprints go in and out of the center, indicating their travels.

Figure 12. The Seven Caves, *Chicomoztoc*, in *Historica Tolteca-Chichimeca* (Early Post-Conquest, Mexico).[18]

At the top of this illustration you see plants and rocks, and at the right, a man wearing a coyote skin and starting a fire. This whole outer rim represents a mountain with seven caves. If you look at the bottom, you see bearded men to the right and men without beards to the left.[17] You know how in cartoons clouds carry the words of the one who is speaking? These men are conversing in the same manner, determined by the wavy lines between them.

Now that we have a better understanding of the people of Mesoamerica and the geographical setting for the Book of Mormon, we will look at some of the more detailed comparisons between Lehi's party and their descendants and the corresponding cultures of Mesoamerica.

CHAPTER THREE

❦❦❦❦❦

Egyptian language and influence on the people of the Book of Mormon

IN ORDER TO UNDERSTAND how the Mesoamerican culture was influenced by the Jaredites, Lehites, and Mulekites, we need to understand the cultures of the Middle East where these three groups came from. The Book of Mormon was written by Nephite men, so we will look at their ancestry in particular, especially Lehi and his sons. What was their occupation in their homeland, and where did they travel before coming to the New World? We also have to ask the question, where did Nephi learn to write in Reformed Egyptian? This was the script for the Book of Mormon throughout its history (see 1 Nephi 1:2; Mormon 9:32–34).

John Tvedtnes, a scholar of Hebrew at Brigham Young University, suggests that Lehi and his sons were metalworkers. The Book of Mormon does not say they sold their wares in Egypt, and one did not have to be a traveling merchant to have a knowledge of the Egyptian writing system. Actually, Egyptian merchants traveled widely, and Lehi and his sons could have picked up the writing system quite easily.[19]

In fact, we know from Mosiah 1:4 that Lehi was taught in the language of the Egyptians. This knowledge was passed on to his sons and all those who kept records in the Book of Mormon. They used the speech of the Hebrew language, but it was written in a modified form of Egyptian. Moreover, the brass plates of Laban were also written in Reformed Egyptian (see Mosiah 1:3–4). The brass plates of Laban contain the books of Moses (similar to the first five books in the Old Testament) and a history of God's dealings with Israel.

Because Lehi and his sons were familiar with Egyptian writing, they would have understood many practices of the Egyptian people. When we look at Lehi's ancestry, Abraham, Joseph, and Moses spent a great deal of time in Egypt. This can be said especially of Moses and the Israelite family that departed Egypt. Egypt's influence did not leave them. Hugh Nibley, an LDS scholar, wrote: "The book [of Mormon] continually refers to the double culture of the people of Lehi: Hebrew to the core, but proud of their Egyptian heritage."[20]

EGYPTIAN ART ON HEBREW JARS

To further substantiate that Egyptian traditions had an influence on Israel, and consequently the people in the Book of Mormon, we can look at a prime example. In the area of modern Israel, over 4,000 ancient clay storage jar handles have been found. Before they were baked to make them firm for storing food or liquid, the soft clay handles were impressed with a stamp seal, many containing a design of an Egyptian winged sun disk and the word *l'melech*, which means "belonging to the king" (see Fig. 13).[21] This was considered a royal emblem of ownership. The Israelites obviously accepted the Egyptian symbol of the winged sun disk for the purpose of showing royalty and power as it did in Egypt, even though the Israelites rejected the false religions of foreigners.

Figure 13. An ancient Hebrew jar handle containing a royal seal with Egyptian design.[21] The Egyptian Winged Sun Disk is portrayed here.

WEIGHING, MEASURING, AND JUDGMENT

We will demonstrate the influence of Egypt on Lehi's descendants, together with their Hebrew ancestry. The eleventh chapter of Alma is significant. Alma 11:1–19 mentions gold and silver being measured along with amounts of grain. For example, "A senum of silver was equal to a senine of gold, and either for a measure of barley, and also for a measure of every kind of grain" (11:7). This is similar to the method the ancient Hebrews used to weigh their grain: "A measure of fine flour was sold for a shekel, and two measures of barley for a shekel" (see 2 Kings 7:16).

The end of Alma 11 tells about Zeezrom, an evil man who was clever with words, who offered Amulek an enormous amount of money if he would deny God. Amulek rejected his offer, rebuked Zeezrom, and taught about God, who would eventually come into the world and redeem his people (see Alma 11:37–40).

After this, Amulek tells Zeezrom that all people will be judged according to their works (see Alma 11:41). The discussion of money at the beginning of Alma 11 is a key to the judgment scene at the end of the chapter, the measuring and weighing of good works, or the lack of good works.

John Sorenson, an anthropologist who taught at Brigham Young University for many years, discussed the measuring of grain in a balance, with a counterbalance of a piece of precious metal. This was an Egyptian practice.[22] You have to imagine a balanced weight system. A pole with a rod at the top holds two suspended bowls. Grain would be placed in one bowl and precious metal in the other. When the grain is at the same level as the metal, they are balanced in the scales.

Why did Alma discuss the Nephite money system, measured grain, and the Day of Judgment in these scriptures? There was wisdom in his writing. Measuring and weighing on a well-balanced scale is similar to the judgment that God will provide to all individuals who lived and died in this world. The scriptures testify of this parallel symbolism. For example, Matthew 7:2 speaks of measuring: "For with what judgment ye judge, ye shall be judged: and with what measure ye mete [measure] it shall be measured to you again." Therefore, it is no surprise that Lehi's people, who initially came from the Near East, carried with them the traditions of their forefathers, and some of these traditions came from Egypt.

A balanced weight system can be seen on the emblem of our U.S. Department of Justice. A blindfolded woman holds a similar weight system to determine the judgment that will be given under the law, which is, ideally, fair and equal to all. The idea of these scales actually came from ancient Egypt.

There are many scenes found in Egyptian funeral art that depict Anubis, a dog-headed god, weighing the deceased's heart on a scale against the feather of truth. The feather, because of its airy composition, symbolized lightness or freedom from guilt.

In our illustration (see Fig. 14a), Anubis holds the symbol of life, the *ankh*, in his left hand. He is seen leading the deceased to the balance scales. At the top of the scale is Maat, an Egyptian goddess who wears a feather on her head that stands for truth, order, and law. Anubis appears again between the scales, and to his right is the beast, Ammut, the destroyer of souls.

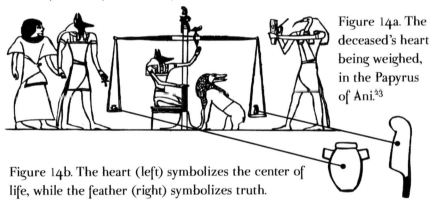

Figure 14a. The deceased's heart being weighed, in the Papyrus of Ani.[23]

Figure 14b. The heart (left) symbolizes the center of life, while the feather (right) symbolizes truth.

On the left, the heart of the deceased is weighed in the balance against Maat's feather of righteousness on the right. The owner of the heart is watching the judgment. If the deceased man's heart is heavier than the feather, the beast Ammut devours him. But if he is successful and has a just heart that balances with the feather of truth, he is led into the presence of his god to live peacefully forever.

To the extreme right of Figure 14a is Thoth, the chief scribe with the head of an ibis bird. He is in charge of recording in his book all that took place with the scales in the hall of judgment. In the scriptures, it is the Lord who is the scribe. We read in Exodus 32:33: "And the Lord said unto Moses, Whosoever hath sinned against me, him will

I blot out of my book." John the Revelator described his vision of the judgment and the opening of these books: "And I saw the dead, small and great, stand before God; and the books were opened: and another book was opened, which is the book of life: and the dead were judged out of those things which were written in the books, according to their works" (Revelation 20:12).

The Lord revealed to Joseph Smith and Sidney Rigdon the kingdoms to which men will be assigned after the judgment, and that all men "shall be judged according to their works, and every man shall receive according to his own works, his own dominion, in the mansions which are prepared" (D&C 76:111).

These comparisons make it clear as to why Alma 11 speaks of measuring in a balance and then preaches about the judgment. The subjects tie in very well because all souls will be weighed and judged by the Savior. Simply put, Alma uses this scenario because it was passed down by his ancestors. After all, Alma, too, was schooled in both the ways of the Hebrews and, in part, the ways of the Egyptians.

CHAPTER FOUR

༺༺༺༺༺༺

Parallels between Hebrew and Nephite festivals

THE NEPHITES HAD THE law of Moses, which was fulfilled when Christ came to minister to them (see 3 Nephi 15:5). They also celebrated Hebrew festivals, as did their ancestors. However, aside from the Book of Mormon account, we have no evidence of these things in Mesoamerican texts or art until the time period after the defeat of the Nephites in AD 385. Because the Apostasy occurred in Mesoamerica in approximately AD 150–200 (see 4 Nephi 1:20), many ceremonies became distorted over time, although there are still similarities that we can identify with those ceremonies of the Israelites.

Festivals in ancient Israel were of extreme importance to the Hebrews. Let's examine the Feast of Tabernacles, or *Sukkot*. Sukkot is a Hebrew word meaning "Feast of Booths." This ceremony resembles the Mesoamerican *Cha-Cha'ac* more than any other performance.

The comparison of the Cha-Cha'ac and the Feast of Tabernacles is extremely important. This is the first time that anyone has compared these two ceremonies in detail. There is a lot of information on both, but they have never been tied together in this manner. The goal of this chapter is to demonstrate that Lehi's party brought traditions with them from Israel to Mesoamerica.

Speaking of the Hebrew Feast of Tabernacles, John Tvedtnes writes, "The original purpose of the feast was probably to pray for rain."[24] The Maya Cha-Cha'ac ceremony had the same purpose: to pray for rain, especially if there was a drought. Tvedtnes also notes that there is a close tie between the crowning of the king and prayer for rain. The year's new agricultural cycle usually had its first rainfall during the Feast of Tabernacles. Tvedtnes also says that Sukkot (the Feast of Tabernacles) was "the reenactment of Yahweh's [Jehovah's/Christ's] enthronement as king of the universe and controller of the elements."[24] The Hebrew king—the symbolic substitute for Jehovah—supervised the activities at the Feast of Tabernacles. Sacrifices were also performed at this feast, demonstrating that atonement is available through the shedding of blood (see Leviticus 17:11).

The Feast of Tabernacles originally celebrated the Clouds of Glory that surrounded the Hebrews after leaving Egypt under Moses' leadership. This festival was similar to our Thanksgiving. Participants thanked God for current and past blessings. We mentioned that the Hebrew name of the Feast of Tabernacles, Sukkot, means "Feast of Booths." The booths (Sukkah) were the structures that were made for the festival (see Fig. 15). After the harvest in autumn, roofs of the booths were constructed out of interwoven green branches with leaves.

Figure 15. Modern Sukkah.

The booths represented the temporary dwellings of their ancestors, who lived in the desert after being led out of Egypt by Moses.

At the Feast of Tabernacles, animal sacrifices were made to God and prayers were offered. This was a time for praying for winter rain, so the world would resume growing crops. To symbolize the hoped-for rain, men encircled the altar and poured water upon it. The Israelites also waved leafy branches, praising the Lord in a spirit of thanksgiving. The purpose of shaking branches was to bring rainfall and subsequently reap successful crops.

We now turn to the Maya Cha-Cha'ac ceremony, which is still practiced today in Yucatan, Mexico. As has been the tradition for hundreds of years, a shaman is in charge of the ceremony. Among the ancient Maya, the king was the shaman (today the Maya have no kings). In a way, a shaman was a priest, although he was not ordained to the same priesthood held by the Hebrews and the Nephites. When a Maya shaman was in charge of the Cha-Cha'ac, he was considered their supreme god, just as the Hebrew king represented God.

In preparation for the Cha-Cha'ac ceremony, an altar was built under the direction of a shaman (see Fig. 16). It was composed of young, leafy branches, corn plants, and gourds that were hung over a table. The top center of this structure is considered a doorway or a portal between our natural world and the Otherworld where the gods live. This "wooden sky," notes archaeologist David Freidel, represents the cosmos, where it is hoped that the rain gods will hear their plea for rain.[25] For a contrast with Hebrew law, it is said that the heavens split on the night of the Feast of Tabernacles. The main feature of these ceremonial structures, with their leafy branches and hanging fruits, are the open roofs. The open roof of the Hebrew and Maya structures was meant to allow the communication of men with their god. It provided a window for the divine presence to observe and be with the people at this joyous occasion.

Figure 16. Modern Cha-Cha'ac Ceremony.

The Cha-Cha'ac altar/table represents the center of the world. The construction itself represents the creation of the cosmos as it existed in the beginning of time. Tvedtnes states, "In a sense, Sukkot symbolizes the creation of the world."[24] Both these ceremonies celebrated the creation, bringing the sacred past into the present.

Food is prepared at the Cha-Cha'ac ritual and is placed on the altar. Gourds filled with pure water are hung from the altar, liquids are sprinkled on the altar, and men circle around the leafy structure."[26]

Similar to the customs of the Hebrews, the Maya shook the arching branches over their altar/table. This represented thunder.

Rain was a very important objective for both the Feast of Tabernacles and the Cha-Cha'ac ceremonies. In both ceremonies, liquid was poured on the altar while the king (Israel) or the shaman (Mesoamerica) prayed for rain. It was at the Feast of Tabernacles in Jerusalem that Christ spoke of the "living water" (see John 7:37–38). The Lord was saying, in so many words, that he was the living water from which all should drink.

We do not know if the Maya ever knew the significance of water in this sense, but the Nephites did. It was Jehovah (Christ) who spoke through the prophet Jeremiah when he said, "They have forsaken me the fountain of living waters" (Jeremiah 2:13). Jeremiah lived in Lehi's time.

Like the Israelites, in the Cha-Cha'ac ritual the Maya made sacrifices to their god. Today, chickens are offered as a sacrifice. It is not known what type of animal (or if humans) were sacrificed anciently. Whatever the case, the shedding of blood was considered necessary to please the gods. When the Cha-Cha'ac ritual was completed, as is similar to the Sukkot, the Maya sat around the table/altar and feasted on the food that was prepared for this occasion. This was a time of joy, whether performed by the Hebrews or the Maya.

Another similarity between these two ceremonies is fire and light. These were important to this ceremony in both the Old and New Worlds. Eric Thompson wrote of the Cha-Cha'ac ceremony: "The difficult entrance and the snakelike movement of the torch-lit procession increase the feeling of awe which attaches to this ritual."[27] The modern Maya also use candles on the altar/table. The Israelites lit oil lamps during the Feast of Tabernacles, and men danced around carrying torches.

It was at the Feast of Tabernacles in Jerusalem where Jesus said, "I am the light of the world: he that followeth me shall not walk in darkness, but shall have the light of life" (John 8:12). It is important to understand the things of nature, such as water and light, and the spiritual significance of these things that points to Jesus Christ. Many times these ancient people did not understand, but those who obeyed gospel principles did. The Nephites understood, as is shown in Mosiah 16:9. Abinadi taught that Christ "is the light and the life of the world; yea, a light that is endless." This scripture was written about 148 BC.

The two festivals considered here were meant for feasting by the people. Loaves of bread, topped with braided ladders representing ladders to heaven, were made for the Feast of Tabernacles. The Cha-Cha'ac ceremony also had bread as part of its festival offerings. But instead of a braid on top of the loaves, the Maya bread was made with many layers of dough, which represented layers of the heavens.[27] The Hebrews also believed that there were many layers to the heavens.

Was the Feast of Tabernacles the inspiration for the Maya Cha-Cha'ac ritual? There appear to be many similarities between the two ceremonies. It is possible that this particular tradition took place after the arrival of Lehi's party to the Americas, the land of promise. It would have had to pass from one generation to the next, perhaps even among the Lamanites through a distorted meaning, as just a ritual for rain.

As John Tvedtnes proposed, it is possible that the Feast of Tabernacles was performed during the time of King Benjamin, as recorded in Mosiah, chapters 2 through 6.[24] The Nephites practiced the law of Moses, which was outlined in the brass plates of Laban. It is clear that the Nephites observed these traditions, and this is verified by the words of Nephi: "And we did observe to keep the judgments, and the statutes, and the commandments of the Lord in all things, according to the law of Moses" (2 Nephi 5:10). They also knew that Christ (Jehovah) gave the law of Moses to them (see 3 Nephi 15:4–5).

Even today the Feast of Tabernacles is well attended. Relatives and friends are invited to the festivities. Tvedtnes takes us through the first few chapters of Mosiah where activities mentioned may point to a Nephite version of the Feast of Tabernacles. Among these activities are the coronation of Mosiah, the gathering of the people at the temple site, the sacrifice of animals for offerings, a tower being constructed for giving speeches to the people, and the giving of speeches. At the Jewish Feast of Tabernacles, words were spoken from ancient records. This bears some similarity to the speech given by King Benjamin. As for praying for rain at the Feast of Tabernacles, Tvedtnes remarks that although King Benjamin does not speak of rain, he does speak of prosperity. Most often, prosperity and rain go hand-in-hand.[24]

One of the main differences between the Feast of Tabernacles and the Cha-Cha'ac ceremony is that the ancient Hebrews not only ate in their temporary booth structures but also slept in them. Today, they just eat their meals in these booths. The Maya, in the Cha-Cha'ac ceremony, did not live under their open framework of branches, but they did eat at the table/altar.

As mentioned, the Feast of Tabernacles goes back to the time of Moses. In the New World, it has been suggested that this festival was performed by King Benjamin's people, as recorded in the book of Mosiah. The Cha-Cha'ac ceremony of the Maya can be traced to approximately AD 500. Two stone vases from Guatemala portray this ceremony date at this time.[25] The Cha-Cha'ac may even have been performed earlier.

To summarize, these are the similar practices of both the Maya and the Hebrews for this ceremony:

1. A structure of four sides was built with the roof made of young branches and leaves. The roof was left open, representing the split heavens (Hebrew) and the cosmos (Maya). For both cultures, building this structure represented the moment of creation.
2. The king/priest (Hebrew) and the shaman/priest (Maya) represented their god and were in charge of the ceremony.
3. Sacrifices were made as an offering to their god for thanksgiving and as a prayer for rain.
4. Men marched around the altar with burning torches, and lights were placed all around.
5. Water was poured on the altar as a symbol of rain.
6. The men shook leafy branches, which symbolized thunder and rain.
7. Bread was made, representing a ladder to heaven for the Hebrews and layers of heaven for the Maya.
8. Both the Hebrews and the Maya feasted on the food prepared and were visited by relatives and friends at this joyous occasion.

The list above makes for a good case that the Maya may have acquired this tradition from the Nephites, who very well may have had a Feast of Tabernacles during King Benjamin's reign. Both the Feast of Tabernacles and the Cha-Cha'ac are still performed today.

CHAPTER FIVE

☙◎◉◎◉◎☙

Mesoamerican knowledge of the Creation

THE NEPHITES kept records on metal plates and possibly other materials, but we have only an abridged version of their history in the Book of Mormon. The Book of Mormon record was kept for us because God knew these scriptures would be another witness of Christ for our day (see Mormon 8:14; 3 Nephi 21; 3 Nephi 23:4). Because Mormon was careful to hide the entire library, except for the record that he gave to Moroni, the teachings were not available to those who remained after the end of the war in AD 385.

We know that not all the Nephites were destroyed (see 2 Nephi 9:53). Those who denied Christ were not killed by the Lamanites (see Moroni 1:2), and many left their Nephite brothers to join the Lamanites (see Mormon 6:15; Moroni 9:24). Others may have allied with the Gadiantons since these robbers had lived among them in previous times (see Helaman 6:18). Perhaps there were even Nephite "draft dodgers." In the end, there were no longer any righteous Nephites except for Moroni. After Moroni's death, the true Nephites became extinct as prophesied by Alma 45:9–11, but their seed still remained as they mixed with other cultures. Whatever the case, some gospel stories managed to seep through to the existing Mesoamerican population as the truth became quickly distorted by apostasy. However, most of these stories are weak imitations of what their ancestors once possessed. The Aztecs, the last great culture to have developed in Mesoamerica, seemed to be aware of the religious heritage that became lost over time. One Aztec poem reads:

> The plumes of the quetzal
> the works of iridescent jade
> all broken and gone
> the memory of a beautiful world,
> god-filled, truth-filled.[28]

The plumes or feathers of the quetzal bird and stones of jade were considered precious. Thus, the Aztecs thought the precious and sacred beliefs they once possessed were now gone. The Aztecs seemed to know there was a time when their people once had this priceless truth and the accompanying "beautiful world."

In Mesoamerica kings and their royal households were educated and could read and write. They were also knowledgeable about religious doctrines. The Maya nobles made grand monuments and painted pottery with detailed scenes that told stories. But the commoners in ancient times spread ideas by word of mouth and through their household art. This was the method by which most traditions passed from one generation to the next. Can you guess what happened?

What occurred was similar to the "telephone game" children play in which one person whispers something into the ear of the person next to him, and that person passes on the message to the next person, until the message has gone all the way around a circle of children. The original message always becomes distorted because it is transferred to more and more people.

This is what happened with stories of the Creation and the gospel principles that were once known by the Nephites. The apostasy, around AD 150–200, was a time of forgetting the true gospel principles. By AD 231, the apostasy was in full swing (see 4 Nephi 1:26–27), but still a small glimmer of truth remained from what the Nephites once knew. If they had remained righteous, this loss of knowledge would not have happened. Also, through their example, we may plainly observe the importance of keeping and using records and scriptures.

We will examine some of the beliefs held by the cultures of Mesoamerica, starting with the belief in a Creator. In LDS doctrine,

God has an eternal companion, and together, they are the parents of all of us. In 1909 the First Presidency of the Church stated, "All men and women are in the similitude of the universal Father and Mother, and are literally the sons and daughters of Deity."[29]

The plates of the Jaredites included an account of the Creation and of Adam (see Ether 1:3–4). The Nephites did not include these things in their writings because they already had this account from the brass plates of Laban, which included first five books of Moses.

The Savior, talking to those whom he visited in the Americas, said that he spoke of "all things, even from the beginning" (see 3 Nephi 26:3). Therefore, Christ reviewed the scriptures from the beginning of time. How wondrous that would have been to have the Creator himself teach you of the Creation. This is what the Nephites had and eventually forgot. Today, Latter-day Saints have two accounts of the Creation—one from Genesis in the Bible and the other from the Pearl of Great Price.

The Book of Mormon does not mention our eternal Heavenly Parents, but chances are that it was a doctrine of the Nephite people. There is much evidence that the Mesoamerican people understood that a supreme creator couple existed. They used different names in various places due to the many languages spoken in the land. Mexican cultures, such as the Aztec, spoke Nahuatl. The Maya spoke several Mayan dialects.

The famous archaeologist, J. Eric Thompson, wrote:

> In Nahuatl [Mexican] mythology, there is a divine pair, male and female. . . . who are the original creators . . . they seem to have given birth to, or created, other gods who later assisted in the creation of the world.[26]

The divine pair was known as Tonacatecuhtli and Tonacacihuatl. They had other names depending on the location, but the more popular set of names for this couple is Ometeotl and Omecihuatl. The Maya had names for their creator couple as well. They were Itzamna and Ixchel, but in a famous Quiché Maya book entitled the *Popol Vuh*, they are called Xpiyacoc and Xmucane. The *Popol Vuh* was written shortly after the Spanish Conquest but is based on an ancient written text. We mention these sets of creator couples because they each have the same function.

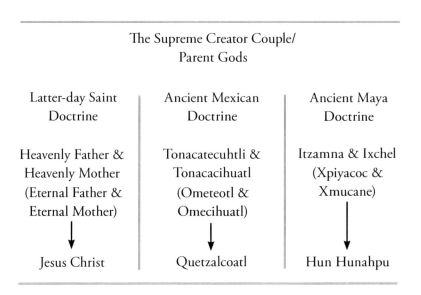

The Supreme Creator Couple/
Parent Gods

Latter-day Saint Doctrine	Ancient Mexican Doctrine	Ancient Maya Doctrine
Heavenly Father & Heavenly Mother (Eternal Father & Eternal Mother)	Tonacatecuhtli & Tonacacihuatl (Ometeotl & Omecihuatl)	Itzamna & Ixchel (Xpiyacoc & Xmucane)
↓	↓	↓
Jesus Christ	Quetzalcoatl	Hun Hunahpu

Each set of divine parents had an exceptional son who was sacrificed and resurrected. These superior and eternal couples were also the creators of the spirits of mankind and sent these spirit children to human mothers. Of course, the mistake they made in Mesoamerica because of the apostasy was that their son is not recognized as the Savior. However, there are some noteworthy comparisons that we will make later between Christ, Quetzalcoatl, and Hun Hunahpu.

The *Popol Vuh*, mentioned above, was written after the Spanish arrived but was taken from a Maya book and from oral traditions that were considered sacred.[30] The stories were told from one generation to the next. Today, the *Popol Vuh* is considered the Bible of the Maya. It is similar to the account in Genesis, starting with the creation of the world. Maya artists painted scenes on pottery and also carved in stone the creation story so their people would understand it.

THE PLANNING OF THE CREATION

We know from the book of Abraham in the Pearl of Great Price that the Gods took counsel among themselves to plan the Creation (see Abraham 4:26). Among the Maya, the Creation involved a council of supernatural beings who discussed and planned the act of creation together.[31] The council of Maya gods is recorded in the *Popol Vuh* and follows a somewhat similar pattern to that described in the Old Testament. They deliberated, agreed, and then united their words and thoughts.

THE CREATION BY WORD

The business of God's "word" is important to Latter-day Saints. The power to do these things is the priesthood. For example, "God said, Let there be light: and there was light" (Genesis 1:3). We know from Moses 1:32 that God's Son, Jesus Christ, created all things. We need to think of Heavenly Father as the architect and his Son as the contractor. They did the planning, and significantly, their "word" carried out the design.

In the *Popol Vuh*, it is remarkable to find a similar situation. A group of gods were involved in the creation, which was executed by their word. Here is some of the translated text from this Maya record:

> Then the earth was created by them. Merely their word brought about the creation of it. In order to create the earth, they said, "Earth," and immediately it was created.[30]

THE PREMORTAL EXISTENCE

In the previous list of divine couples, each couple is considered married and the creators of spirit children. In the Pearl of Great Price, Moses 6:51 reads, "I am God; I made the world, and men before they were in the flesh." You cannot have a father of children without a mother. Today, the vast majority of conventional Christians do not believe in an existence before life on earth. Latter-day Saints have this knowledge because of the restored gospel.

The Nephites understood the premortal state, though the Book of Mormon only speaks of it in a roundabout way, referring to the beginning as "from the foundation of the world" (Alma 13:3). Helaman 14:17 refers to the premortal state when it says, "But behold, the resurrection of Christ redeemeth mankind, yea, even all mankind, and bringeth them back into the presence of the Lord." If men are to be brought "back into the presence of the Lord," they must have been there before.

Ancient Mesoamericans knew and understood that men came from a divine creator couple. An Aztec poem reads:

> . . . beyond, happiness exists.
> Or is it that we come to earth in vain?
> Certainly some other place is the abode of life.[32]

Eduard Seler, a German archaeologist, researched traditions of the heavenly pair in Mexico and found that one of their primary functions was to create the spirits of mankind. The creators were the great initiators of life and sent souls to occupy the bodies made by human procreation. The celestial creator gods also gave warmth and breath to the infant before birth.[33]

In the Mexican picture book *Borbonicus Codex*, a child descends from its heavenly home to a mother (see Fig. 17). The footprints show the direction that the child is going. At the bottom of this scene, which is not included in our illustration, the head of the child appears as it is being born.

The Maya also understood this concept. For the Maya, "to touch the earth" was an expression for birth when the child came from heaven to the earth. Douglas Gillette, a specialist in comparative religions, said that it was "an ancient Maya doctrine of the preexistence of the soul, a soul that is far more ancient and enduring than the brief span of our lifetimes on earth."[66] This is a marvelous religious tradition that explains so well the idea that is unique to the LDS Church in the modern world.

Another example may show a child's descent from heaven to its mother (see Fig. 18). Garth Norman, a Latter-day Saint archaeologist, suggests the earliest

Fgure 17. A Child descends to its mother, *Borbonicus Codex* (Early Post-Conquest Mexico).[33]

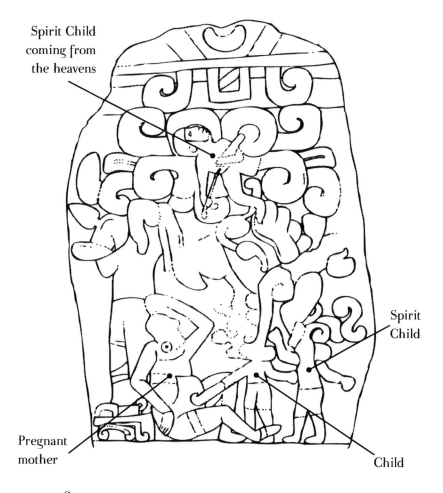

Spirit Child coming from the heavens

Spirit Child

Pregnant mother

Child

Figure 18. A spirit child descends from heaven to its mother, who has an umbilical cord connected to the child. Stela 10, Izapa, Chiapas, Mexico (about 200 BC).[34]

illustration of the premortal state is found on a carved upright rock monument. Called Stela 10 and found at Izapa, Chiapas, Mexico, this monument was made in approximately 200 BC.[34] Here we see a child floating above a reclining figure with a swollen belly. The spirit child above is coming from the heavens to enter its earthly mother's womb. Two children are to the right of the mother figure. One child is holding a scepter-like rod, possibly symbolizing an umbilical cord attached to the mother. Perhaps the other child is the same child as the spirit child. Among the Maya, it was not unusual to portray the same individual more than once in a scene as being in various stages of an event.

QUETZALCOATL, THE MAIZE GOD, AND CHRIST

In our chart of the Supreme Creator/Parent Gods on page 38, we see that Heavenly Father and Heavenly Mother's son was Jesus Christ. In many respects, Christ may be viewed in Mesoamerica as the Mexican god Quetzalcoatl or Hun Hunahpu, the Maya maize (corn) god. Like Christ, Quetzalcoatl was considered the creator of the world, along with his divine heavenly father, Tonacatecuhtli,[33] who was known among the Maya as Itzamna, the father of the maize god.

In one story, Quetzalcoatl is responsible for separating the sky from the earth. The gods in Mexico hold various duties, and as a result, they sometimes have different names to go along with the task they perform. In this case, Quetzalcoatl is called Ehecatl-Quetzalcoatl. He looks strange with his bird-like beak mask, which represents the device with which he blows his divine breath (compare to Ether 2:24). Ehecatl-Quetzalcoatl lifts the sky and separates it from the earth (see Fig. 19).[35] The top band design represents waters of the heavens, while the lower portion of this band contains stars. Beneath Ehecatl-Quetzalcoatl's feet is the earth.

Another version tells of Quetzalcoatl turning into a World Tree (which LDS scholars believe to be the Tree of Life) and accomplishing the same task of separating the sky from the earth.[36] The maize god of the Maya, Hun Hunahpu, sets up the World Tree (the Tree of Life) in the middle of the universe, separating the "lying-down-sky" from the

Figure 19. Ehecatl-Quetzal-coatl, Mexican god of air, lifts sky from earth, *Seldon Codex* (Pre-Conquest, Mexico).[12]

earth.[3] In a way, the story is the same in the Bible (see Genesis 1:6–8). The waters on the earth were divided by the atmosphere above. We will talk much more about Quetzalcoatl's and the maize god's roles compared with Christ's role in the following chapters.

QUETZALCOATL VERSUS TEZCATLIPOCA

All mankind are our brothers and sisters, but two sons of our Heavenly Parents affect our spirituality the most. They are Christ and Lucifer. We are all aware of the decision each made, one for good and the other for evil (see 2 Nephi 2:17–18).

Lucifer, whose name literally means "light bearer" or "shining one," held this name in the premortal state before he rebelled against our Heavenly Father. After he was dismissed and cast down to the earth, he became known as the devil or Satan. Because of his former name of Lucifer, we know that he once held authority in the premortal life. However, when it came to this earth, he did not play a role in its creation (see D&C 76:25–27), even though the ancient Mexicans thought he may have.

With that said, we will now turn our attention to a deity in Mesoamerica who has some of the characteristics of Lucifer/Satan. His name is Tezcatlipoca. Tezcatlipoca's brother was Quetzalcoatl, and they were rivals from the beginning.[37] For the most part, Tezcatlipoca was the opposite of Quetzalcoatl. He was dark and destructive and the author of chaos, while Quetzalcoatl was a figure of light and mankind's helper.[38]

It is said that Tezcatlipoca attempted to take possession of the newly created earth.[39] As a result, a great battle between Quetzalcoatl and Tezcatlipoca took place in the heavens. If we compare Tezcatlipoca with Satan, we can look to Moses 4:3 in the Pearl of Great Price to tell us the story. Heavenly Father said, "By the power of mine Only Begotten [Christ], I caused that he [Lucifer/Satan] should be cast down."

In Mesoamerica, legends say that Quetzalcoatl hit Tezcatlipoca with a club, knocking Tezcatlipoca from the heavens and down into the waters of the earth. When Tezcatlipoca was cast out, his foot was ripped off as he was being thrown out of heaven (see Fig. 20). This story may be compared to Revelation 12:7–9. Tezcatlipoca's foot was replaced by a smoking mirror, through which he saw a

Figure 20. Tezcatlipoca loses his foot when he is cast down to earth. From *Codex Vaticanus* (Pre-Conquest, Mexico).[40]

dark future for mankind (see Fig. 21).[40] This may be symbolic of Satan's own misery and desire to share darkness and sorrow with all mankind (see 2 Nephi 2:18).

Tezcatlipoca also had some good qualities, just like Lucifer did before he rebelled. Mesoamericans believed that their world contained paired opposites. Examples are water and fire, life and death, and light and dark. Many times, Tezcatlipoca was seen as the dark side of life, even as a destroyer. Other times, he was seen as a god of creation. In general, Tezcatlipoca represented negative forces. This would include war and hostility, sickness, deceitfulness, swindling and stealing, vanity and greed, and discord of all kinds.[41]

Tezcatlipoca was not necessarily viewed by ancient Mexicans as evil, but rather as a contrast to Quetzalcoatl. One could not exist without the other. Just as the Latter-day Saints of today, the ancient Mexicans believed that there is opposition in all things (see 2 Nephi 2:11).

Figure 21. Tezcatlipoca
with smoking mirror
for a foot, *Borgia
Codex* (Pre-Conquest,
Mexico).[50]

Smoking mirror

left
foot

CHAPTER SIX

ᄋᄋᄋᄋᄋ

Adam and Eve and Mesoamerican legends

THE STORY OF THE FALL of Adam and Eve was recorded on the brass plates that were in Laban's possession (see 1 Nephi 5:10–11) and on the gold plates made by the Jaredites (see Ether 1:4). It was a blessing that the Nephites were able to obtain both of these records. This information would have been passed to Lehi's children and down through their righteous descendants, since it is critical in appreciating the need for a Savior.

Before the Spanish arrived in 1519, stories of the Mesoamerican creation and the first ancestral parents were passed orally among the natives to their offspring. After the Spanish Conquest, these legends were recorded by Spanish clergymen and by the Indians themselves if they had learned to read and write Spanish. Since there are several of these stories coming from different places and times, we can be reasonably sure they are authentic. In other words, they are not stories simply taken from the Bible when the Catholic Spanish brought it with them from Spain to the Americas.[50]

We also have Mexican codices that portray the story of the first parents, and many of those codices were made before the arrival of the Spanish. In the legends that the native Indians told to the Spanish, each Mesoamerican location has a different name for Adam and Eve, but the stories are the same. The myths relate that the Supreme Couple created a garden for the first couple. This garden was called Tamoanchan or Tollan in most sources, and it is nearly identical in description with the Bible's Garden of Eden.[42]

The stories tell generally of Eve, for which the Mexicans had various names (Xochiquetzal, Ixnextli, Tlazolteotl-Ixcuina, Itzpapalotl, and Oxomoco). To simplify matters, we will use the name of Xochiquetzal (see Fig. 22). Legend has it that she transgressed, and this transgression brought death into the world and altered both her and her husband's lives.

Xochi means "flowers"

Food offering

Figure 22. Xochiquetzal, the Mesoamerican Eve, *Borgia Codex* (Pre-Conquest, Mexico).[100]

Instead of eating the fruit of the tree of knowledge of good and evil as recorded in Genesis, Xochiquetzal cut a blossom from the sacred tree in the garden. In Mesoamerica, everything is considered living. The tree bled after being wounded when Xochiquetzal plucked a flower from its branch (see Fig. 23).

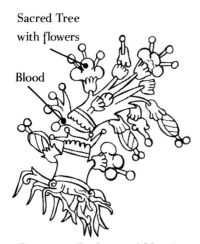

Sacred Tree with flowers

Blood

Figure 23. Broken and bleeding tree in Tamoanchan, *Codex Telleriano-Remensis* (Early Post-Conquest, Mexico).[43]

Breaking a flower from the tree signified death. Death was unknown in their wonderful garden of Tamoanchan.[42] In Alma 12:23, we understand that if Adam and Eve had not eaten of the fruit of the tree of knowledge, they may have eaten of the fruit of the Tree of Life. If they had done so, they would have lived forever in Eden and never tasted death. This would have prevented the life of all of humanity. But, as we know, their transgression was necessary to fulfill the plan of our Heavenly Father.

Tezcatlipoca, disguised as an animal, deceived Xochiquetzal and persuaded her to pluck a flower from the forbidden tree. Tezcatlipoca, as you recall, may be equated with Satan. To punish Xochiquetzal and her husband, the Supreme Creator Gods banished them to the earth (see 2 Nephi 2:18–19 for a comparison). They could no longer enjoy their wonderful garden.[42]

In Mesoamerica, when the first couple came to earth, something different and unexpected happened to them. They had a great deal of knowledge before they left the garden. They could remember everything of their life in Tamoanchan, so the supreme creator couple caused that they would not be able to see as clearly as they had before. The Maya book, the *Popol Vuh*, tells this part of the story:

> Their eyes were merely blurred by Heart of Sky [the Creator].
> They were blinded like breath upon the face of a mirror. Thus
> their eyes were blinded. They could see only nearby; things
> were clear to them only where they were. Thus their knowledge
> was lost.[30]

Consequently, this couple lost their former wisdom when they were cast out of the garden. In other words, they could not remember the things that took place before they left the garden; they had been struck with divine amnesia. Their eyes became blurred, which may be compared to 1 Corinthians 13:12: "For now we see through a glass [archaic English for "mirror"], darkly; but then face to face: now I know in part; but then shall I know even as also I am known." Ixnextli is another of the names for the Mesoamerican Eve. In English her name translates as "eyes blinded with ashes," which refers to the same event.[42]

Mexican codices depict the fall of man from paradise. Figure 24 is a typical illustration. The German scholar Eduard Seler interpreted this scene as the first man plunging down from his home in paradise to the earth. The blindfolded man to the right is the same person. The blindfold shows that he is guilty of a transgression. The blindfold may also have another meaning. The first man's eyes were blinded from the smoke and ashes, so he could not see clearly. The other image to the bottom left is the heavenly staircase, which the Mexicans used to demonstrate the first man falling, as though down a set of stairs, from his home in paradise.[33]

Figure 24. Tamoanchan (Paradise), the House of Descent, *Borgia Codex* (Pre-Conquest, Mexico).[99]

We are reminded of William Wordsworth's poem:

Our birth is but a sleep and a forgetting;
The soul that rises with us, our life's star,
Hath had elsewhere its setting,
And cometh from afar;
Not in entire forgetfulness,
And not in utter nakedness,
But trailing clouds of glory do we come
From God, who is our home.[44]

In the Maya area of Quintana Roo, Mexico, there is a myth from the distant past about a rope, which was a pathway that joined the earth with the sky. It was a lifeline, almost like an umbilical cord that linked the two worlds, connecting the natural world to the heavens.[45] This link was severed at the time of the Fall, when earth and heaven were separated from one another. Since a separation occurred, it was necessary that specific steps be taken to reunite both body and spirit with their heavenly home. Birth, death, and resurrection are all components of this process.

Chapter Seven

ⓢⓢⓢⓢⓢⓢ

Mesoamerican knowledge of birth, death, and resurrection

THE VARIOUS CULTURES that lived in Mesoamerica understood a great deal about birth, death, and resurrection. However, many of these beliefs were twisted and altered from the knowledge that the Nephites had hundreds of years before. We will attempt to tell those parts that are similar to gospel principles and acquaint you with the way they may have deviated from the truth.

We already discussed the premortal state of mankind, which is a firm belief among Mesoamerican cultures. They knew, as seen in the Aztec poem below, that life was short in their sojourn on earth and that they would eventually return to their heavenly home. The Aztec poem reads as follows:

> Let us consider things as lent to us, oh, friends;
> only in passing are we here on earth;
> tomorrow or the day after,
> as Your heart desires, oh, Giver of Life,
> we shall go, my friends, to His home.[32]

REBIRTH AND BAPTISM

Passages in the Book of Mormon have numerous references to baptism that make it clear how this ordinance should be performed.

But by the end of the Nephite era, gospel principles were drifting into a state of apostasy. In an urgent letter to his son Moroni, Mormon wrote:

> And after this manner did the Holy Ghost manifest the word of God unto me; wherefore, my beloved son, I know that it is solemn mockery before God, that ye should baptize little children. (Moroni 8:9)

Little children do not need to repent because they do not have a full knowledge of what they are doing (see Moroni 8:10). In other words, little children do not have the ability to choose whether or not to accept the baptismal covenant. It is difficult to imagine a five- or six-year-old understanding the concept of right and wrong, let alone covenants. For this reason, baptizing a child would have no meaning. However, this is exactly what the Nephites were doing before the close of the Book of Mormon.

When the Spanish arrived a little more than one thousand years later, this practice was still performed by the Aztec and Maya people. The Spanish saw this ritual with their own eyes and actually thought this form of baptism was the work of the devil since it was too similar to the way they baptized their own infants. Isn't it amazing that this form of apostasy occurred in both the New and Old Worlds? Satan labors tirelessly that we may set "at naught the atonement" of Christ (see Moroni 8:20).

The *Madrid Codex*, drawn by the Maya before the Spanish arrived, has several illustrations of infants and small children being baptized by sprinkling water over their heads (see Fig. 25). This was a form of baptism without the proper authority. By this time, the

Figure 25. A woman sprinkles a child for baptism, considered a purification rite, *Madrid Codex* (Pre-Conquest, Maya).[98] (Blocking on chest done for respect.)

Mesoamericans considered it a ritual way of purifying their infants, and women usually performed the act.[46]

The Mayan word for baptism was *zihil,* which literally means "to be born again." The Maya believed that by doing this ceremony, the infant received a purer nature and was protected in the future against evil. They did this sprinkling between the ages of three and twelve years old.[47] "To be born again" is the exact phrase used in the scriptures (see Alma 5:49; John 3:3) and is a popular phrase used by many conventional Christian denominations today.

In Mesoamerica, the design of a shell symbolized a mother's womb, among other things. Almost everything was symbolic to them, as we have seen before. There are several illustrations in the codices that show people coming out of a shell submerged in water. Does this refer to baptism and to being "born again" through immersion? It might. A German scholar and an interpreter of Figure

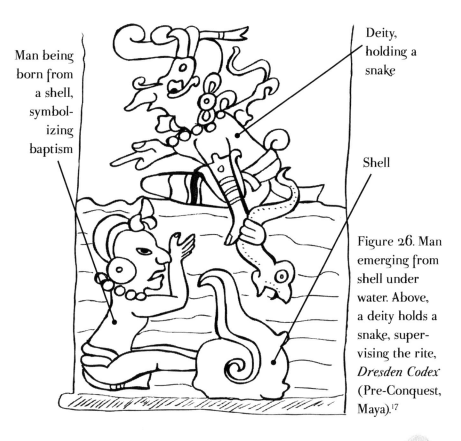

Man being born from a shell, symbolizing baptism

Deity, holding a snake

Shell

Figure 26. Man emerging from shell under water. Above, a deity holds a snake, supervising the rite, *Dresden Codex* (Pre-Conquest, Maya).[17]

26 believed that "just as the [shell]fish issues from the shell, so emerges man from the womb of his mother."[48] The Mesoamericans believed their salvation was in the water.[46]

Another fine example is from the *Codex Nuttall*, painted in Oaxaca, Mexico, before the Spanish Conquest (see Fig. 27). Since shells were considered symbolic of birth, this may very well be a rite of baptism, and if so, depicts the proper method of being immersed in water, as in Figure 26. We do not know whether this ceremony refers to baptism, but it most certainly refers to purification. When you are purified, you are able to start your life anew, like a newly born child.

The concept of rebirth is significant. We know from Romans 6:1–12 (see also Colossians 2:12–13) that being immersed in the water represents death, and that coming out of the water represents rebirth or resurrection. This rebirth has the same elements of physical birth, which are water, blood, and spirit (see Moses 6:59).

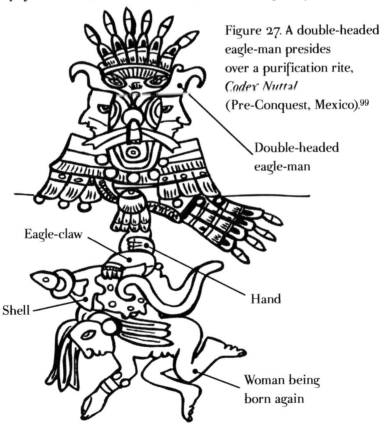

Figure 27. A double-headed eagle-man presides over a purification rite, *Codex Nuttal* (Pre-Conquest, Mexico).[99]

Double-headed eagle-man

Eagle-claw

Hand

Shell

Woman being born again

DEATH

Deceased Children

This subject brings joy, gratitude, and hope to those who have lost a child under the age of eight. As far as we know, there are no other people who believe that a special place is assigned to deceased children except for Latter-day Saints and the Mesoamericans. This is another powerful connection between the Book of Mormon and the people of Mesoamerica.

The Book of Mormon makes it clear that children who die before the age of accountability are redeemed through Christ and are considered "alive in Christ" (see Moroni 8:10–12), because they are innocent and sinless. Their destiny is eternal life, which is the celestial kingdom (see Mosiah 15:25; D&C 137:10).

It is often circulated in the Church that during the Millennium, righteous parents will be able to raise their deceased children. Orson Pratt, an early LDS apostle, said:

> I am of the opinion that the spirits of children who die here regain their former dimensions of manhood or womanhood [as they were in the premortal state]. . . . But by and by the resurrection will come, then these full-grown spirits, who have died in infancy here, will again enter into the infant tabernacle, and they will come forth as infants, as they were at the time they laid down their bodies; then their parents will have no difficulty in recognizing them.[49]

It is truly amazing when we compare this belief with that of the Mesoamericans. There are some differences, but it's basically the same concept. Some of the early Spanish clergy wrote about the natives' beliefs about the death of children. In Mesoamerican belief, the Heavenly Creator Couple thought of these deceased children as "precious stones" or "jewels."[50] In 3 Nephi 24:17, Heavenly Father refers to his righteous children as "jewels." Why would this heavenly couple cast their precious jewels away to limbo or hell?

Referring to the same doctrine, there is an illustration in the Mexican *Codex Rios* that depicts deceased children (see Fig. 28). The children who have passed away are sitting under a fruit-bearing tree. The fruit drips milk to nourish the children. Now read what a non-LDS researcher has found among the myths of the people who made this drawing:

> These deceased infants were extremely important to the fate of the human universe, because, in the future, when the current great world age came to an end . . . their spirits would leave the tree and return to repopulate the earth.[35]

Fruit dripping
with nourishment

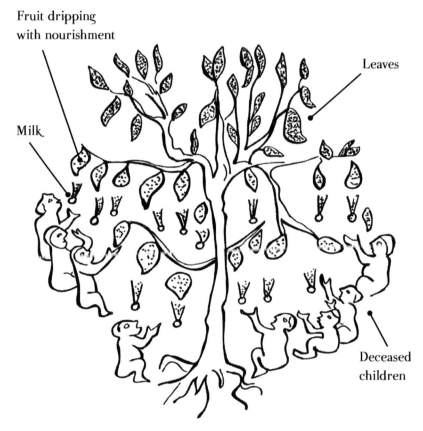

Leaves

Milk

Deceased
children

Figure 28. Deceased children receiving milk from the fruit of the tree in Tamoanchan (Paradise), *Codex Rios* (Early Post-Conquest, Mexico).[35]

Deceased Adults

In the ancient world, burying the deceased meant returning the body to the womb of mother earth, the place where people expected to be reborn (see Mormon 6:15). The same concept is expressed in Job 1:21:

"Naked came I out of my mother's womb, and naked shall I return."

The shape of a mother's womb is similar in the art of the Middle East and Mesoamerica. It is simply a U-shape. Sometimes the Mexican codices show a *U* to mean a grave, which is actually considered the womb of the earth (see Fig. 29). In our illustration, a skull lies in the U-shaped grave, while the person to be buried is wrapped with cloth (at the right of the illustration) in what is referred to as a "death bundle." Both the skull and the dead individual are the same person. This technique of duplicating the person in a scene was a frequent technique in Mesoamerica, as was mentioned earlier (see Figures 18 and 24).

Yokes are used on oxen to pull a plow, but the yokes in Mesoamerica were different. The Mesoamericans sometimes put a U-shaped stone yoke in the burial chamber of the deceased. Stone yokes were designed after leather and wood yokes. Ball players used fabric, wood, and leather yokes as protection around their waist (see Fig. 30). The Mesoamerican ballgame was played for over two

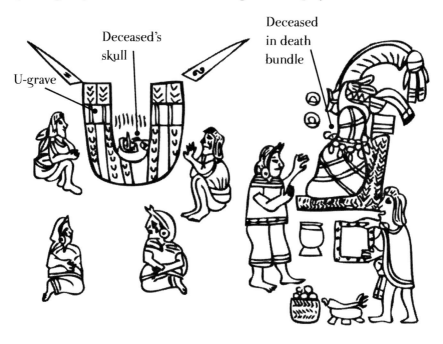

Figure 29. Left: a U-shaped grave; Right: death bundle. *Codex Magliabecchi* (Early Post-Conquest, Mexico).[12]

Yoke

Figure 30. Maya ball player wearing a yoke and padding, Panel 7, Yaxchilan, Chiapas, Mexico.[31]

thousand years (that's quite a run considering most of our sports have only been around for one to two hundred years). These yokes acted as a safety measure, just as a mother's womb protects a child before it is born.

Unlike leather yokes for the ballgame, stone yokes were too heavy to wear. Stone yokes were obviously made to last throughout generations of time as pieces of religious art (see Fig. 31). Placing a stone yoke with the deceased in a grave may have the meaning of lying in the womb before the individual would be reborn. On a clay vessel from Mexico, a U-shaped device is drawn around a man (see Fig. 32). There has also been an archaeological report of a burial where a body was found lying full length with the head placed inside one of these yokes.[51]

An interesting discovery was made in a cave tomb at Jerusalem (see Fig. 33): stone headrests that date to the seventh century BC. This is near the time that Lehi and his party left Jerusalem. It was customary for the head of the deceased to lie within the U-shaped stone, symbolizing what some scholars believe to be a return to the comfort of the mother.

Figure 31. Ceremonial stone yoke, Veracruz, Mexico.[12]

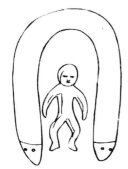

Figure 32. U-shaped serpent surrounds man on Mexican vessel.[12]

This would then mean a hope for rebirth and the resurrection of the deceased.[52]

In addition to the U-shaped stones, many other artifacts that served diverse purposes were buried with the deceased. Those born of royalty in Mesoamerica had several items surrounding their body that were to be used for their journey into the afterlife. Common items were furniture, pots and bowls with food, jewelry, and weapons of war. Weapons were thought to be necessary in case the deceased came across an evil spirit on the other side.[12] They did not want to be caught defenseless in spiritual warfare on the path to the heavenly realms.

The Egyptians did exactly the same thing. They wanted to be prepared for their journey in the otherworld, as they called it. Much food and fine clothing were put into the tombs. Cosmetics were even buried

Figure 33. Stone headrests on burial benches of St. Etienne cave tombs, Jerusalem, 7th Century BC.[52]

with women who apparently wanted to look their best on the other side. Figures of slaves were also buried in anticipation that these objects would help the deceased in death as they had in life.

The Book of Mormon discusses resurrection, particularly in Alma 11:37–46 and 12:12–18. The Egyptians, Mesoamericans, and especially the Nephites before the end of their great nation all believed in the resurrection. It was an important doctrine among these people.

RESURRECTION

You can see from the above discussion that everything about burial in both Mesoamerica and Egypt was geared toward a belief in the resurrection. Who but the living would require food and makeup? We will mention some other artifacts that have to do with the deceased getting to the afterlife that were buried with the dead. Reaching the other side of the veil, as we would say, is called rebirth or resurrection. Of course, this will happen when our bodies are reunited with our spirits at the appointed time.

The scriptures inform us of different degrees of glory in the heavens (see 1 Corinthians 15:40–41; D&C 76). Each kingdom can be likened to the sun, the moon, or the stars. So, you could say that the brilliance of the highest kingdom is brighter than the lowest kingdom. Daniel 12:3 refers to the resurrection of the dead when he writes of the righteous as stars: "And they that be wise shall shine as the brightness of the firmament; and they that turn many to righteousness as the stars for ever and ever."

The Aztecs told Sahagun, a Spanish priest, of their belief in the different levels of the heavens that they went to when they died and that life was but a dream (similar to Jacob 7:26). They said of their dead:

> They did not die but woke from a dream they had lived . . . and became once more spirits or gods. . . . They said, too, that some were transformed into the sun, others into the moon, and others into various planets.[16]

Perhaps the Maya understood this to some extent as well. They believed that their ancestors became stars too. They also had the idea that when a person died, he not only became a star, but the better the person, the bigger the star.[48]

One of the best symbols of the resurrection in ancient times was the sun. The sun goes across the sky, sinks in the west, and comes up each morning in the east. That is how we see the sun, but that is not the way the ancients viewed the sun. They were a little more imaginative than we are. The ancients saw the sun going across the heavens like a bird, giving warmth to the crops and making them grow, and then at the day's end, dying in the west. At night the sun, particularly in Mesoamerican thought, went to the underworld and became the moon. In the morning, the sun rose triumphantly and was reborn in the east. For this reason, rulers in Egypt and Mesoamerica compared themselves to the sun, especially in light of the resurrection.

Can we relate to this? John Taylor, a president and prophet of The Church of Jesus Christ of Latter-day Saints, wrote in 1852:

As surely as we look in the east for the rising of the sun in the morning . . . so surely will 'the Sun of righteousness arise with healing in his wings' [Malachi 4:2], so surely will the sleeping dead burst from their tombs.[53]

Let us examine one particular object that was sometimes buried with the dead both in the Middle East and in Mesoamerica that has something to do with the deceased's journey and eventual resurrection. This also has to do with the sun.

Francis Gibson, who lived among the Maya and studied their ways, found that the symbol of the wheel was of religious importance to them. In remote areas of Guatemala, many still walk and choose to carry heavy loads rather than use a wheeled cart. Gibson asked the Maya why they still do this after having been exposed to wheels for over four hundred years. Their response was that the wheel was a symbol of the ancient sun god and thus was considered a sacred symbol.[54]

First of all, let us explain about the wheel in Mesoamerica. Wheels would have been made of wood, and wood disintegrates with time. There are no illustrations in Mesoamerican art that show wheels, and there are no remains of life-sized wheels. This has been a criticism of the Book of Mormon. If Lehi's people and the Mulekites came from the Middle East, why are there no wheels in Mesoamerica? There may have been wheels during the days of Book of Mormon peoples, but we need to understand what the symbol of the wheel meant to later generations in Mesoamerica. One of the symbols of the wheel was definitely the sacred sun.

Mesoamericans did have the wheel. Years ago archaeologists discovered many small, clay-wheeled objects in Mesoamerica. At that time, these scholars thought that they were toys. It is hard to believe that the natives did not know how to make a life-size cart if they knew how to make a small one. Many toys today are miniature replicas of real, life-sized items. Today most archaeologists acknowledge that these clay, wheeled animals were used for funeral ceremonies.

As time has progressed, more and more of these ancient wheeled animals have been discovered buried with both children and adults (see Figs. 34 and 35). In most cultures, adults are not usually buried with "toys," which suggests these wheeled animals had a special significance for the Mesoamericans. In addition, scholars have found that Mesoamericans knew five ways to attach an axle, which indicates they also had technical knowledge of the wheel.[55]

Many of these old, wheeled animals have a rosette decoration on the wheel (see Figs. 36 and 37). A rosette is a flower design, and in Mesoamerica it specifically refers to the sun. In fact, flowers in general represent the sun. In Maya, the hieroglyph for the sun contains a flower. In Mesoamerica, all the wheeled animals represent the sun in some way. Dogs, jaguars, deer, and monkeys are all associated with the sun. For example, Figures 38 and 39 show the monkey with an associated sun sign.

Wheeled creatures were also put in ancient graves in Mesopotamia and Persia (see Figs. 40 and 41).[56] This is the area where the Jaredites most likely lived before they came to the Americas. These wheeled animals were about the same size as those found in Mesoamerica and are believed by scholars to be part of the funeral ceremonies.

Left: Figure 34. Wheeled dog with tubes to house axels, Tres Zapotes, Veracruz, Mexico.[55] Right: Figure 35. Wheeled deer from Cihuatan, San Salvador.

Left: Figure 36. Wheeled monkey on platform with sun wheels.
Right: Figure 37. Wheeled jaguar with sun wheels. Veracruz, Mexico. [57]

Sun

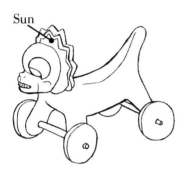

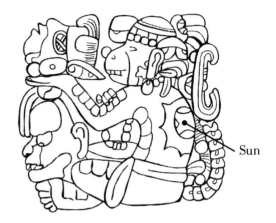

Sun

Above: Figure 38. Wheeled
Spider Monkey with a sun
headdress, Mexico.[57]
Right: Figure 39. Monkey
with sun on back, Yaxchi-
lan, Chiapas, Mexico.[14]

Below: Figure 41.
Limestone lion on
platform wheeled
cart, Susa, Persia.[56]

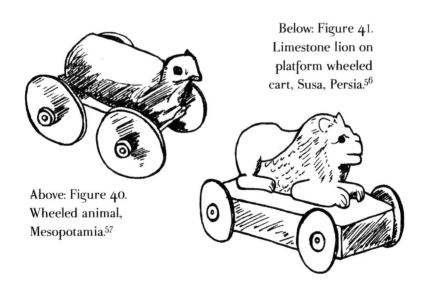

Above: Figure 40.
Wheeled animal,
Mesopotamia.[57]

The few wheeled creatures that have been found in Mesopotamia do not have rosettes on their wheels. However, the rosette was clearly a symbol of the sun in ancient Mesopotamia and in other places in the Near East (see Figs. 42 and 43). The concept of being resurrected like the sun after its nightly journey through darkness was a traditional belief in both the Middle East and Mesoamerica. Ceremonies involving wheeled animals may represent vehicles used by the dead on the road to resurrection that all must travel.

Much more will be discussed about resurrection in the chapter dealing with Quetzalcoatl, the Maya maize god, and Jesus Christ.

Left: Figure 42. Near Eastern sun design, Philistine.[57] Below: Figure 43. Winged sun disk, Syria.[58]

Sun

CHAPTER EIGHT

〽〽〽〽〽〽

Quetzalcoatl and Jesus Christ

IF THE PEOPLE of Mesoamerica truly were the remnant of the Book of Mormon civilization, evidences should be found of faith in Jesus Christ, even if in apostate form. The major gods in Mesoamerica that are the most like Christ are the Mexican deity Quetzalcoatl and the Maya maize god called Hun Hunahpu in the *Popol Vuh*. We will look at some of the stories about Quetzalcoatl and also explain why it is difficult to separate which portion of the legends may refer to Christ and which stories are about one of the other Quetzalcoatls.

That's right! There was more than one Quetzalcoatl. Just as people today take on the name of Mohammed, the famous prophet of the Muslims, and many Latinos use the name Jesus, in like manner some men throughout Mesoamerican history were named after their god, Quetzalcoatl. Using the name of a royal ancestor or even a god made men appear powerful and gave them authority as a leader.

There are two kinds of information about Quetzalcoatl. On the one hand we have the writings that were recorded by the Spanish conquerors and their priests of the Catholic Church. These writings contain stories that the Indians told the Spanish about the things that had happened in their past. The other source of information we have on Quetzalcoatl is contained in artworks of clay and stone and pictures in the codices.

Figure 44. Feathered Serpent, Pyramid of Quetzalcoatl, Xochicalco, Morelos, Mexico.[17]

Let us begin with the literal translation of the name Quetzalcoatl, because this is how he is shown in most works of art. *Quetzal* means "Quetzal bird" and *coatl* means "serpent." For this reason this god is commonly referred to as the "Feathered Serpent" (see Fig. 44). The Quetzal bird, which has beautiful long green tail feathers, is related to the heavens because it flies. Snakes, which crawl on the ground, are associated with the earth. This leads us to the man–god duality of Quetzalcoatl.

It has been suggested that Quetzalcoatl was thought to have a heavenly father and an earthly mother, making him half man, half god. In this sense, we can see the association with Jesus Christ, who was God the Father's son as well as Mary's, a mortal woman. Some scholars believe that the traditions of a half-man, half-God are quite ancient, even though it is oftentimes difficult to separate the men named Quetzalcoatl from the original god Quetzalcoatl.

There are also other reasons the Feathered Serpent may relate to Christ. In 2 Nephi 25:20, we read the story of the brazen serpent that Moses lifted up on a pole to heal the Israelites who were bitten by poisonous serpents. In the same verse, Nephi makes a comparison to Jesus Christ. This too has been suggested as a reason the serpent symbol may refer to Christ, or Quetzalcoatl, in Mesoamerica. We will come back to the subject of the Feathered Serpent after we discuss some other things about Quetzalcoatl.

We mentioned that there were many Quetzalcoatls. One of the most well-known men in Mesoamerica was a prophet and leader named Topiltzin Quetzalcoatl. Much is written about him after the Spanish Conquest. A problem is that Mesoamericans had a habit of mixing the past with the present. They believed that everything in history repeats itself. In other words, when we read that Quetzalcoatl promised to return to his people, we don't know if it was Topiltzin Quetzalcoatl who promised to return, or if it was the god Quetzalcoatl/Christ who said he would return, or if both of them said that they would return. So it is really impossible to determine who said what—the original god Quetzalcoatl/Christ, the man Topiltzin Quetzalcoatl, or both.

It would be easy to say that the undesirable traits of Quetzalcoatl belong to one of the men by the same name and that all the desirable traits belong to the god Quetzalcoatl. For example, some of the stories refer to crimes that Quetzalcoatl committed, such as drunkenness, fornication, and murder.[59] We would assume that these crimes were committed by a man named Quetzalcoatl, not the god Quetzalcoatl. Some of the legends that seem to refer to the god, not the man, are stories of his virgin birth and the story that he turned into the planet Venus. These things appear to obviously refer to Christ, but as we shall see, they need examination.

Scholars estimate that Topiltzin Quetzalcoatl lived sometime between AD 700 to 1000.[59] Leon-Portilla, a specialist in ancient Mexican cultures, believes that the god Quetzalcoatl existed a thousand years before Topiltzin Quetzalcoatl.[60] That would place the god Quetzalcoatl in the right range, close to AD 33–34, when Christ visited the Americas after His resurrection.

There are various accounts of Topiltzin Quetzalcoatl's birth. Most of these stories relate that his mother's name was Chimalma, that she died in childbirth, and that the child Quetzalcoatl was raised by his grandparents. Some writings say that Chimalma was a virgin, and others give her a husband. In the virgin stories, the Creator God, Tonacatecuhtli, sent a messenger to Chimalma, telling her that she would have a boy child, that he would be miraculously born, and that he would have a full sense of reason.

Once again, here is the problem. The Spanish texts were written almost 1,500 years after Christ visited the people of the Book of Mormon. By AD 200, the seeds of apostasy were underway. Thirteen hundred years is plenty of time for the true gospel and story of Christ to become distorted. In addition, the Spanish Catholic clergy added Christian doctrine to the words of the native Indians. So, we don't know if Topiltzin Quetzalcoatl used the story of the virgin birth of the god Quetzalcoatl/Christ or if the Spanish decided to include that part of the biblical story in the history of this ancient people.

Another story about Topiltzin Quetzalcoatl is that when he left his people and died, he turned into the planet Venus.[59] For this story, it is tempting to say that this Quetzalcoatl was Christ, because Christ was also referred to as Venus. Venus is often called "the bright and morning star," and there is a scripture in Revelation 22:16 that refers to Christ as such: "I Jesus have sent mine angel to testify unto you these things in the churches. I am the root and the offspring of David, and the bright and morning star." However, this scripture is from the New Testament and is not in the Book of Mormon. Therefore, the Nephites may not have understood the concept of Venus, the morning star, relating to Jesus Christ. There is always the possibility that Christ was associated with Venus by the Nephites, but we do not have knowledge of that in the Book of Mormon abridgement.

Apparently, none of the Quetzalcoatls were linked to Venus until the history of Topiltzin Quetzalcoatl. These legends state that upon his death, Topiltzin Quetzalcoatl rose to heaven and became the Morning Star. This is how he became resurrected, deified, and associated with Venus.[61] Venus also became tied with events of war among the people of Mesoamerica. In fact, a Maya hieroglyph of Venus over a shell has been interpreted as signifying "star wars."[2]

The Feathered Serpent is also associated with war and Quetzalcoatl. Christ may very well have been called the Feathered Serpent among the Nephites. We simply do not know. The Feathered Serpent is a type of Quetzalcoatl. We know that feathers and birds represent the heavens, and serpents were considered wise in the ancient world. Matthew 10:16 even reads: "Be ye therefore wise as serpents, and harmless as doves." Also, the serpent appears to have a *new* body after it sheds its skin. This is why the serpent represents resurrection to the Mesoamerican community.

Perhaps you have seen the Pyramid of the Feathered Serpent in Teotihuacan, or a picture of it. Teotihuacan is about twenty-five miles from Mexico City. It is one of the largest cities built in Book of Mormon times, starting about 300 BC. This famous pyramid, also called the Temple of Quetzalcoatl, was built around AD 200, when the church of the righteous saints started to collapse as recorded in the Book of Mormon (see 4 Nephi). The Pyramid of the Feathered Serpent is a graphic example of what happened at this point in time. In fact, non-LDS scholars acknowledge this era in Mesoamerica around AD 200 as the beginning of a collapse with many destroyed or abandoned cities. It wasn't until the end of the fourth century that cities began to expand and become powerful again.

Figure 45. Feathered Serpent head, Pyramid of the Feathered Serpent, Teotihuacan, Morelos, Mexico.[65]

There were many contentions among the Lamanites and Nephites. We cannot ignore the symbol of the Feathered Serpent being adopted by the Lamanites after their defeat of the Nephites when they set up their own religious doctrines. The Pyramid of the Feathered Serpent has dozens of stone heads of the feathered serpent attached to the exterior (see Fig. 45).

An incredible burial site was found in the 1980s underneath the Pyramid of the Feathered Serpent. Approximately 200 human victims were found tied and bound, sacrificed, and buried as a dedication ceremony for the pyramid.[62] From this point on, around AD 200, the Feathered Serpent was associated with war. We will show an illustration from a Mexican codex to emphasize this point. Figure 46 portrays a Feathered Serpent with a knife in his tail, which he uses to sacrifice enemies. He is seen devouring a sacrificial victim with stab wounds.

Sacrifice was common throughout Mesoamerica, for worshipers truly believed that through death (and sacrifice) comes life. In a roundabout way, this may form a parallel to

Figure 46. Feathered Serpent with knife in tail devours a sacrificial victim, *Codex Telleriano-Remensis* (Early Post-Conquest, Mexico)[43]

Christ's atoning blood, which is for the benefit of all mankind (see Jacob 4:4–5). However, the apostasy destroyed any true meaning of sacrifice among these ancient people (see Mormon 4:14–15, 21).

As already stated, the Lamanites may have adopted the Feathered Serpent and turned him into their war emblem, which was a common thing to do in Mesoamerica. But, we need to note that there are good accounts of the Feathered Serpent in the *Popol Vuh*. One part of the text states that the Feathered Serpent is one of the creator gods among the Quiché Maya. This supernatural deity is known as Gucumatz (Quetzal Bird Serpent) and is the same as the Mexican Feathered Serpent, Quetzalcoatl. Gucumatz is in no way related to war and sacrifice, only creation. The *Popol Vuh* mentions this supernatural personality only briefly, although his role is crucial in the creation.[30]

We will now move on to the qualities that most likely refer to the legends of the god Quetzalcoatl. These stories appear to refer to Christ as he was known in Book of Mormon times, although they are somewhat altered. We will also refer to the Maya maize god, whose name in the *Popol Vuh* is Hun Hunahpu. The maize god is illustrated on clay vases, bowls, and plates. There is even a mural in Guatemala, painted about 100 BC, portraying the maize god.[63] (See the appendix of this book for more information on the Maya maize god.)

It is important to include the maize god of the Maya when comparing the gods of Mesoamerica to Christ, who was also known as the Bread of Life (see Moroni 4:3; John 6:51). You can make a type of corn bread from maize. The maize god took part in the creation, was sacrificed, died, and was resurrected—similar to Christ. We will therefore compare various accounts of Hun Hunahpu with stories of Quetzalcoatl and Christ.

We already talked about the god Quetzalcoatl raising the sky from the earth (see Fig. 19). In Maya hieroglyphs at Palenque, Chiapas, Mexico, there is a statement that the maize god performed the same act of creation that Quetzalcoatl did; that is, he separated the sky from the earth.[31] The maize god did this when he positioned the Tree of Life at the center of the universe. There is a Mexican text written after the Spanish Conquest that says that Quetzalcoatl turned into a tree to push the sky up from the earth, and this is nearly the same idea.[64]

SACRIFICED FOR MANKIND

For Christ also hath once suffered for sins, the just for the unjust, that he might bring us to God, being put to death in the flesh, but quickened by the Spirit: By which also he went and preached unto the spirits in prison. (1 Peter 3:18–19)

The story of Quetzalcoatl saving mankind was written after the Spanish conquistadors arrived in Mexico; however, some of the codices, drawn before the Spanish arrived, depict the same thing. To briefly relate the Mexican myth, Quetzalcoatl descended to the underworld to shed his blood on the bones of the deceased so that they would live again.[64]

The entire legend, with all its strange details, sounds odd to the Christian world. But Latter-day Saints know of the truth of the saving work of Jesus Christ, which is alluded to in the scripture above. In verse 20 of Peter 3, the scripture explains that these were the spirits of those who had been waiting since the days of Noah. 1 Corinthians 15:22 states that *all* men will be resurrected as a result of Christ's sacrifice. These two teachings are important in understanding this myth.

To make a long story short, there is an ancient Mexican story about a great flood similar to the story of Noah in the Bible. Everyone died in the flood except for a small family. Mesoamericans consider everything before the flood another age in their history. They also believed that after the flood, a new age started, and this is the one in which we live in today.[50]

Quetzalcoatl went to the underworld to retrieve human bones after the great flood destroyed the world and its people, who were considered "the ancestors." A goddess ground the bones of the ancestors like corn and placed the flour-like meal in a container. Quetzalcoatl performed a bloodletting ritual and dripped his sacrificial blood on the ground bones, giving them new life. The Indians believe they are the descendants of these ancestral bones.

There is a picture in the *Borgia Codex* that illustrates part of this story. Quetzalcoatl is acting as the god of breath and air, so he wears the red beaked mask through which he blows his divine breath of life

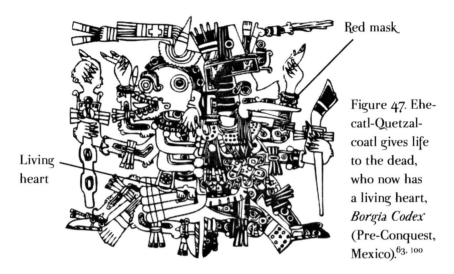

Red mask

Living heart

Figure 47. Ehecatl-Quetzalcoatl gives life to the dead, who now has a living heart, *Borgia Codex* (Pre-Conquest, Mexico).[63, 100]

into men (see Fig. 47). In this capacity, his name becomes Ehecatl-Quetzalcoatl. We saw him separating the sky from the earth in Figure 19. Ehecatl-Quetzalcoatl is a Mesoamerican god of creation, the god who gives of his sacrificial blood willingly to save mankind, and the god who is responsible for rebirth or resurrection.

In Figure 47, Ehecatl-Quetzalcoatl is back to back with a skeleton. Quetzalcoatl already sacrificed his blood and gave it to the deceased, and now the skeleton lives. You can see the living heart hanging down from the skeleton's ribcage. This is a clear sign that the deceased will be reborn. The ancient Mexican people believed that the dead deserved to be brought back to life because of Quetzalcoatl's blood sacrifice.[32]

It has been suggested by some Latter-day Saint scholars that this particular illustration represents the above story as told to the Spanish by the Mexican Indians. The *Borgia Codex* was drawn before the Spanish arrived, and once again, the story was recorded in writing after the Spanish came to the New World.

Although the ancient Aztecs believed that there were many gods who sacrificed themselves for mankind, they did realize that because of their sacrifice, men will live again. Another ancient Mexican poem reads:

It was the doctrine of the elders
that there is life because of the gods;
with their sacrifice, they gave us life.[32]

THE RESURRECTION

And by the power of the Father he [Christ] hath risen again,
whereby he hath gained the victory over the grave; and also in
him is the sting of death swallowed up. (Mormon 7:5.)

It is the Maya maize god who celebrates the story of the
resurrection. Numerous pieces of clay pottery show his story of
rebirth. The *Popol Vuh* tells the legend of Hun Hunahpu, the maize
god, whose head was hung on a tree after being sacrificed[30] (see Fig.
48). Taking into consideration that one of the symbols of the earth
was a turtle, in this picture painted on a Maya bowl we see the maize
god resurrecting from the split shell of a turtle (see Fig. 49).

Below: Figure 49. The Maya Maize
God resurrects from a turtle shell,
which represents the earth (interior of a ceramic bowl).[70]

Above: Figure 48. The head
of the Maize God on a Maya
vase, Museum Popol Vuh,
Guatemala.[12]

A wonderful example of resurrection can be seen on a stone lid used for the sarcophagus of Pakal, the great Maya king of Palenque, Chiapas, Mexico (see Fig. 50). On this famous lid, Pakal wears the turtle shell as a pendant necklace, giving reference to the maize god's resurrection. Scholars are in agreement with this

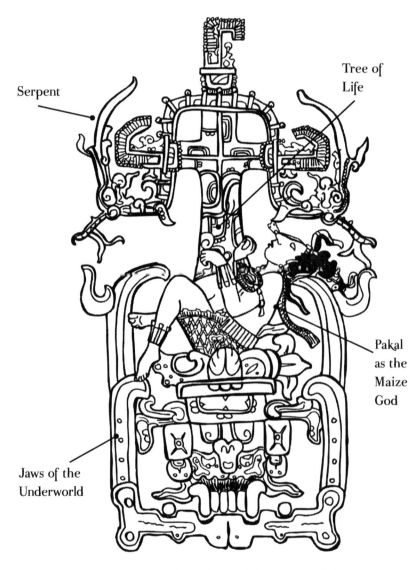

Serpent

Tree of Life

Pakal as the Maize God

Jaws of the Underworld

Figure 50. Sarcophagus lid of King Pakal as Maize God, Palenque, Chiapas, Mexico.[17]

theory. As Douglas Gillette says, the cosmic turtle shell allows "the Resurrection Body to soar up from the realm of death into the world of eternal life."[66] Pakal is seen as the young maize god with the Tree of Life springing from his body in resurrection. He is posed in what is referred to as the "birthing position," the position of a child in the process of being born, symbolic of bringing new life to himself.

In Babylonian and Assyrian cultures, as well as other areas of the Near East, large earthen jars were often used to bury the deceased. In order to accommodate the interior structure of these jars, knees were drawn up, placing the body in the desired fetal position. This is symbolic of a future rebirth when the individual is born anew from the womb-like enclosure.[12]

The sarcophagus of Pakal has Mesoamerica's most famous stone carving. On this sarcophagus is depicted the story of the Tree of Life, the maize god, and the resurrection. The bony U-shape at the bottom of this design represents the jaws of the underworld, where we find the womb of the earth. In addition, the sides of Pakal's sarcophagus depict his ancestors rising from their graves, each sprouting from a fruit-bearing tree.[30] The sides and the top of the sarcophagus demonstrate the defeat of death and victory of the resurrection.

Deity, Light, and the Sun

When Christ visited the people in the New World, we can only imagine the brightness of his coming, both figuratively and literally. His arrival brought rejoicing, healing, and light. Joseph Smith described his being as one "whose brightness and glory defy all description."[67] As recorded by Nephi, his father, Lehi, saw Christ in a vision of the future where Christ is described as "descending out of the midst of heaven, and he [Lehi] beheld that his luster was above that of the sun at noon-day" (1 Nephi 1:9).

The scriptures do not specifically say that when Christ appeared to the people (see 3 Nephi 11) he descended from the clouds as a personage with light emanating from his being, but the Lord announced to the people, "I am the light and the life of the world." Christ wore a white robe and on another day of his visit radiated a white light to his twelve disciples (see 3 Nephi 11:11, 8; 19:25, 30).

In the sixteenth century, a Catholic friar named Juan de Cordova wrote the following account while working with the Zapotec Indians of Oaxaca, Mexico. Quoting the Indians, he recorded:

> On the day we call Tecpatl a great light came from the northeastern sky. It glowed for four days in the sky, then lowered itself to the rock . . . in the Valle [Valley] in Oaxaca. From the light there came a great, a very powerful being, who stood on the very top of the rock and glowed like the sun in the sky. . . . Then he spoke, his voice was like thunder, booming across the valley.[68]

The above story may be related to an account in the *Popol Vuh* of the first dawn, which describes the bright light as a man. Dennis Tedlock's translation follows:

> The sun was like a person when he revealed himself. His face was hot, so he dried out the face of the earth. Before the sun came up it was soggy, and the face of the earth was muddy before the sun came up. And when the sun had risen just a short distance he was like a person, and his heat was unbearable. Since he revealed himself only when he was born, it is only his reflection that now remains. As they put it in the ancient text, "The visible sun is not the real one."[69]

These citations illustrate that a being of great light, comparable to the sun, made a great impression on the natives of the New World. It is no wonder that these ancient people related this personage to the living sun.

An association of Quetzalcoatl with the sun may be seen in the *Borgia Codex* (see Fig. 51). Here this creator god has the design of the sun on his back. We should also consider a story that was written after the coming of the Spanish. The god Nanahuatzin, an aspect or feature of Quetzalcoatl, became the sun. This god is pictured first as a sickly being who jumped into a fire pit after a ritual fast, which resulted in his emergence as Tonatiuh, the sun god of the Aztecs.[70] It should also be considered that Nanahuatzin sacrificed himself for the well-being of mankind.

Because parts of the picture that we have painted here may be questioned, Latter-day Saint scholars need to use caution when approaching the intriguing and mysterious figures of Quetzalcoatl and the Maya maize god in their attempts to draw connections between these deities and the resurrected Jesus Christ. Nevertheless, there is sufficient evidence for us to connect these stories together and give a bit of acceptance to them.

Breath and wind mask

Sun

Figure 51. Ehecatl-Quetzalcoatl as god of wind, air, and breath, with symbol of the sun on his back, *Borgia Codex* (Pre-Conquest, Mexico).[100]

CHAPTER NINE

࿐࿐࿐࿐࿐

The Tree of Life in Mesoamerica

IN THE BOOK OF MORMON, the Tree of Life is first mentioned in the vision of Lehi (1 Nephi 8, 11, and 15). The Tree of Life, or the World Tree as it is sometimes called in other cultures, was not only important to the Mesoamerican community but also to those in the ancient Middle East. We will discuss both areas since Lehi's party, and even the Jaredite culture, certainly had an impact on traditions in ancient Mexico and Central America. They had an influence because they brought many traditions with them from across the sea. One tradition in particular is the Tree of Life.

What exactly is the symbolism of the Tree of Life? We find in the Book of Mormon that Nephi asked the Lord the meaning of his father's vision of the Tree of Life. After Nephi was given the same vision as Lehi, he understood. The Lord revealed the meaning to him, and this revelation is recorded in 1 Nephi 11:

> And behold this thing shall be given unto thee for a sign, that after thou has beheld the *tree* which bore the fruit which thy father tasted, thou shalt also behold *a man descending out of heaven*, and him shall ye witness; and after ye have witnessed him ye shall bear record that it is the Son of God. (1 Nephi 11:7; emphasis added)

Then, a small phrase in the scriptures says the proverbial thousand words: "It [the Tree of Life] is the love of God" (see 1 Nephi 11:21–22). John 3:16 reads:

> For God so loved the world, that he gave his only begotten Son, that whosoever believeth in him should not perish, but have everlasting life.

The Tree of Life is none other than Christ himself. Our Savior was the greatest gift and expression of love from God to mankind.

Early European Christian paintings of Christ show him with the Tree of Life.[71] Sometimes in these pictures the Lord is actually crucified and hanging on the Tree of Life. In fact, Acts 5:30 states that Jesus was killed and hung on a tree. In these paintings of Christ with the Tree of Life, Christ's sacrificial blood is considered the fruit of the tree.[72] The sacrifice of the atonement of Christ makes the resurrection possible, which in a sense is the gift of the fruit of the Tree of Life.

The Tree of Life was considered the center of the world, and to Christianity, Christ is the Tree of Life. It is interesting to note that other ancient religions had their dying and resurrecting gods who represented the Tree of Life. For example, in Egypt it was Osiris, in Rome it was Attis, in the Nordic countries it was Odin, in ancient Mexico it was Quetzalcoatl, and for the Maya it was the maize god.[71]

The Tree of Life in the Near East

Memory of the Garden of Eden and its Tree of Life was not lost in the generations following Adam and Eve. Their descendants may not have completely understood its meaning, but they did know that the Tree of Life was tied to the concept of rebirth and that it represented the center of the world when the Earth was formed.

One of the earliest examples of the Tree of Life in the Near East is a seven-branched tree accompanied by two birds (see Fig. 52).[71] This illustration is on a stone vase from Khafje, Mesopotamia, and dates to before 3000 BC. The same design was used by the Hebrews for their Tree of Life, which became the Menorah (see Fig. 53). The Menorah is a seven-branched candlestick that is still used today by Jews, and its history of use goes back to the time of the temple

Figure 52. Early Tree of Life on vase, Mesopotamia, about 3000 BC.[71]

in ancient Israel (see Exodus 25:31–40).[73] The flaming lights of the Menorah represented the fruit of the Tree of Life,[72] as well as the light and life of Jehovah. Jehovah is the God of the Old Testament whom Latter-day Saints identify as Christ.

Did you notice the birds on either side of the seven-branched Tree of Life in Figure 52? The birds represent heavenly guardians of the Tree of Life because of the nature of their wings, which are associated with the heavens. Almost two thousand years later in the ninth century BC, the subject matter of the sacred tree and bird guardians remained the same. Sometimes bird-headed cherubim (celestial beings) with wings guarded the Tree of Life (see Fig. 54).[74] At other times there were at least two men or angels guarding the tree, while the bird image is perched at the top of the Tree of Life (see Fig. 55).[75]

Figure 53. The Jewish seven-branched Menorah.

Figure 54. The sacred Tree of Life attended by bird-headed guardians, Assyria, Mesopotamia, about the ninth century BC.[74]

Figure 55. Assyrian Tree of Life with winged guardians, Mesopotamia.[75]

THE TREE OF LIFE IN MESOAMERICA

Let's see how the Mesoamericans portrayed the Tree of Life. There is only one portrayal of the Tree of Life discovered in ancient Mexico that has bird guardians. It was found in Izapa, Chiapas, Mexico. We will discuss this illustration in stone shortly.

Most Tree of Life themes in Mesoamerica have three fixed elements: (1) the Tree of Life, (2) two guardians, and (3) a bird at the top of the tree. Oftentimes there are four trees representing the four quarters of the earth (north, south, east, and west) and one major tree at the center of the universe. This sacred tree of the center is thought to have its branches in the heavens, its trunk on the earth, and its roots in the so-called underworld. One of those directional World Trees from ancient Mexico can be seen in the *Codex Fejervary-Mayer* (see Fig. 56).

Maya portrayals of the Tree of Life were very decorative in comparison to Mexican motifs of the same (see Fig. 57). Even though these two cultures of Mesoamerica exhibited the World Tree differently, the theme was nearly identical. These concepts were like peas in a pod with those of the Near East.

A Mesoamerican illustration of birds guarding the Tree of Life is from Stela 5, Izapa, Chiapas, Mexico (see Fig. 58).[72] Stela 5,

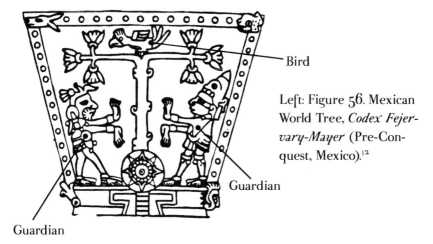

Bird

Left: Figure 56. Mexican World Tree, *Codex Fejer-vary-Mayer* (Pre-Conquest, Mexico).[12]

Guardian

Guardian

Bird on World Tree

Guardian

Guardian

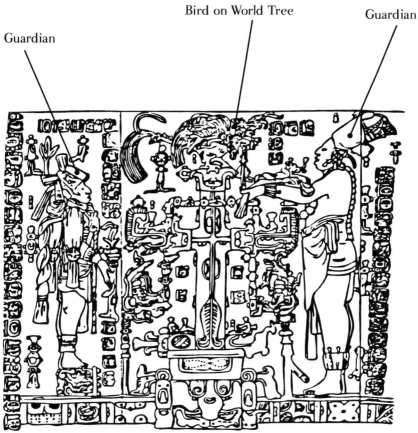

Above: Figure 57. Maya World Tree, Palenque Chiapas, Mexico (plate XLI, Bull. 28, Washington DC: Bureau of American Ethnology).

discovered in 1941 by the Smithsonian Institution and the National Geographic Society, dates to 400 BC, which is prime Book of Mormon time, right around the time of Enos and Jarom. This carving in stone is what many Latter-day Saints call The Tree of Life Stone. There are hieroglyphic images among the figures in this fascinating narrative story in stone. It is difficult to interpret the meaning of these hieroglyphic images, but they are currently under study. We will look at the individual carved objects and figures, which are better understood and have interpretations.

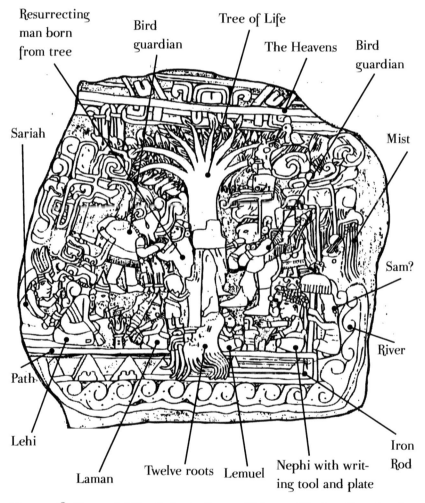

Figure 58. Tree of Life, Stela 5, Izapa, Chiapas, Mexico. Drawing by Garth Norman. Identifications added.[72]

This important carving in stone contains the major elements referred to in Lehi's dream or vision of the Tree of Life, which occurred about 600 BC (see 1 Nephi 8:10-35). It helps us to understand a possible way in which some of the symbolism came to the Americas. Latter-day Saint archaeologists do not completely agree with the interpretation of this stela,[76] but even so, there appear to be strong parallels between the design of Stela 5 and similar themes found in the Near East. These elements are the tree and its fruit, roots that penetrate into the underworld, branches with birds that reach into the celestial heavens, and guardians of the Tree of Life.[72]

The figures and symbols of Stela 5 in Figure 58 are marked with arrows pointing to their possible identification corresponding to Lehi's vision of the Tree of Life. Most of the interpretation has been done by LDS scholar Garth Norman.[72]

Pay particular attention to the figure to the left who appears to be coming out of the tree. In a sense, we saw a similar design on Pakal's sarcophagus lid (see Fig. 50). Remember that his ancestors were portrayed coming out of trees, as well as Pakal himself, who has the World Tree rising from his body. These are resurrection scenes.

On Stela 5, the individual coming out of the tree apparently is in the process of being resurrected and has the fruit of the Tree of Life in his hand. It is the fruit of the Tree of Life, a gift of God through his Son, that will give resurrection, immortality, and especially glory to those who follow him. Lehi described the fruit of the Tree of Life as "most sweet" (see 1 Nephi 8:11).

In all fairness to LDS scholars who do not support the idea that this stela derives from Lehi's vision, we will quote John Clark's article, "A New Artistic Rendering of Izapa Stela 5: A Step toward Improved Interpretation":

> If it does not show Lehi's dream, what does it show? . . . The scene shown has cosmic significance; the heavens, the earth, and the underearth are conventional framing features for earlier art in this area. So is the tree—the World Tree that is considered in Mesoamerican thought to grow at the center of the earth, from whose surface it reaches up to heaven and down to the underworld.[76]

The Species of the Tree of Life

It must be noted that the World Tree is not an apple, pomegranate, olive, or any one particular type of tree. It may be a variety of things. For example, in Mesoamerica the World Tree is sometimes a crocodile tree, the ramon (bread nut) tree, the ceiba tree (the largest in Mesoamerica), the Nance tree (where the maize god's head was hung), a cacao tree (the source of chocolate, and considered sacred), or even a maize plant (corn is also considered sacred).

In Figure 59, the crocodile tree has a bird in its branches. The man-made tree staff, held by the maize god's son, also has a bird at the top. Both trees are considered the World Tree of creation. The *Popol Vuh,* written more than 1,500 years after this illustration was made in Izapa, may record the story in part.[30]

Figure 60 depicts the World Tree as the maize tree. This illustration is from an ancient Mexican codex. You can see the typical bird at the top of the tree. The tree itself springs from the swirling primeval waters of creation. Not shown in our partial illustration are two deity guardians giving their blood to the sacred maize World Tree.

It is not so unusual for there to be so many species that are identified as the Tree of Life in Mesoamerica. In the Near East, the Tree of Life has been called a cedar, sycamore (fig tree), oak, almond, olive, or cypress tree. In other words, no specific kind of tree has been named to clearly identify the Tree of Life that existed at the beginning of time in Paradise.

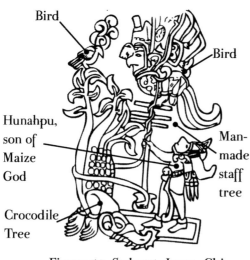

Figure 59. Stela 25, Izapa, Chiapas, Mexico (about 200 BC).[34]

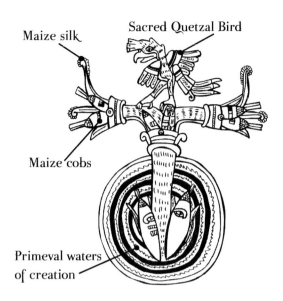

Maize silk

Sacred Quetzal Bird

Maize cobs

Primeval waters
of creation

Figure 60. The
World Tree as a
maize tree, rising
from the waters of
Creation, *Borgia
Codex* (other fig-
ures not included
in illustration)
(Pre-Conquest,
Mexico).[100]

KINGS ASSOCIATED WITH THE TREE OF LIFE

People, and especially kings, have been associated with trees
throughout ancient history. For example, in the book of Daniel in
the Old Testament, King Nebuchadnezzar told Daniel of his dream
of a cut-down tree. Daniel interpreted the king's dream, saying that
the tree represented the king and that the cutting down of the tree
represented Nebuchadnezzar disgraced by his people because of
his own actions. It was not until a seven-year period passed that
Nebuchadnezzar resumed his kingship after he came to know God
(see Daniel 1–5).

It is important to note that the scriptures indicate Christ is the
King of Kings (see 1 Timothy 6:15; Revelation 17:14). Strange as it
may seem, earthly kings of the ancient worlds of Mesoamerica and
the Near East chose to associate themselves symbolically with the
Tree of Life, which was believed to be at the center of the world.
Many kings thought that if they wore a costume with Tree of Life
symbols, they literally became the Tree of Life and the center of the
world. What king would not want that?[12]

The idea of the king being the center of the world, as well as the
Tree of Life, goes back to the Olmec civilization in Mesoamerica.
Remember, the Olmec are a good candidate for the Jaredites. We

Figure 61. Olmec portraying a ruler as a World Tree, surrounded by four small corn plants, which represent the corners of the earth. Arroyo Pesquero, Veracruz, Mexico.[77]

have two illustrations from the Olmec concerning the Tree of Life. Archaeologist Kent Reilly has determined that Figure 61, carved on a piece of jade, represents a ruler as the World Tree at the center with four maize seeds at the corners representing the four trees at the corners of the world. Maize corn even sprouts from the top of his head.

This concept existed for almost two thousand years in Mesoamerica, right up to the time when the Spanish conquistadors arrived. Reilly interpreted another carving showing an Olmec ruler with a bound maize design on his apron, and believes that this king also represents the World Tree (see Fig. 62).[77]

Kings wore Tree of Life leaves and branches in their headdresses.[12] Among the Maya, this concept advanced to a costume with branches of the World Tree on the apron, and sometimes with leaves (see Figs. 63 and 64). You will notice the face on the apron in Figure 63.[77] This is because the Mesoamericans viewed their sacred Tree as having a living and divine spirit. What this costume meant is that both the Tree and the king were not only divine but were the center of the universe.

Since the Tree of Life was personified with the king at the center of the Mesoamerican world, one of the titles of the Maya kings was *Yahau te*, meaning "Tree Lord." In fact, a Maya vase has a text reading "his becoming the tree," which Dorie Reents-Budet, a Mesoamerican art historian, suggests refers to the king's role

Figure 62. Olmec ruler with bound maize on center of apron, Puebla, Mexico.[77]

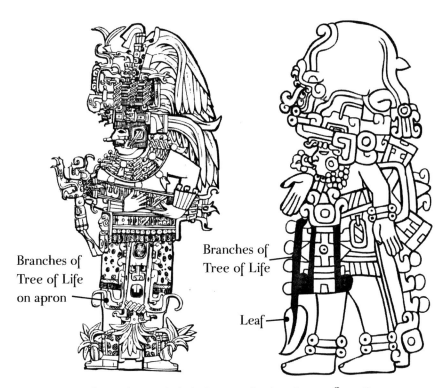

Branches of
Tree of Life
on apron

Branches of
Tree of Life

Leaf

Left: Figure 63. Stela 10, Seibal, Guatemala, dated to AD 849. Courtesy of Dover Publications.[78] Right: Figure 64. Branches and leaf on apron of ruler, Stela 6, Cerro de las Mesas, Veracruz, Mexico.[79]

as the World Tree. Other vases describe rulers as the "standing one tree-person" and "holy tree person."[80] The Maya king was literally believed to be the World Tree in the flesh.[3]

If the idea of the king as the Tree of Life began with the Olmec as we noted, and since the Olmec are the Jaredites who came from the Old World at the time of the Tower of Babel, then there should be evidence that Mesopotamian kings represented the Tree of Life as well. Many examples of this further link Mesoamerica with the Old World, the latter-day testament with the old and the new.

Simo Parpola, a Middle Eastern specialist, writes: "From the earliest times on, Mesopotamian kings had been portrayed as living personifications of the cosmic tree."[81] A picture of the king, growing out of the first mountain of creation in ancient Assyria, sprouts and holds branches of the Tree of Life, while sprouts arise from his loins (see Fig. 65).

Figure 65. King as Tree of Life, rising out of the first mounain of creation, from Assur (Assyria).[81]

And like the Maya, Mesopotamian kings bore names that identified them as the Sacred Tree.[81] Sometimes in art the Mesopotamian king stood between two winged guardians, implying that he was the Tree of Life. Furthermore, the Mesopotamian king wore a ceremonial dress embroidered with gold stars and with the sacred Tree of Life.[81] This concept was also used by the rulers of the Maya in their clothing.

Sometimes ancient kings of the Near East were shown holding a scepter (a rod that was an emblem of royalty). These scepters bore leaves, branches, or flowers. According to Geo Widengren, a Near Eastern scholar who wrote a book on kings and the World Tree, this branch was believed by the people to be the twig Adam cut from a branch of the Tree in Paradise.[82] Even pharaohs of Egypt sometimes wore a collar of greenery to indicate their function as the Sacred Tree.[83]

Apparently the same enduring tradition existed in other parts of the Old World. In the eighth century AD, King Charlemagne was portrayed with the World Tree on his apron, a tradition carried down from ancient times (see Fig. 66).[84]

During the Apostasy, doctrinal imitations replaced true concepts. Perhaps the kings of the world wanted to usurp the power of the King of Kings, since they wanted

Figure 66. Charlemagne wearing an apron of the Tree of Life.[84]

to imitate divinity. As you recall, the true King of Kings is a title of Jesus Christ, whose symbol is the Tree of Life. People of the ancient world often believed their kings were divine. This was true of both some parts of the Middle East and Mesoamerica. Even Nephi, a prophet from about 23–20 BC, was thought to be a god by some Nephites who didn't understand the gospel principles (see Helaman 9:41).

The Tree of Life, or World Tree, was known from the days of the Garden of Eden in paradise. Unfortunately, the true meaning of the Tree of Life and its relationship to Jesus Christ became obscured over the years by most religions. Even so, it is important to know that the concept of a Tree of Life remained from the beginning of time and that the tradition was brought from the Old World to the New World.

The sacred World Tree has always carried the idea of life and resurrection. Even today in Santiago Atitlan, Guatemala, the Maya bury their dead with a small mound of earth placed on top of the grave. On top of the mound they plant a tree, which represents the deceased's rebirth.

CHAPTER TEN

ⓒⓒⓒⓒⓒⓒ

The Hill Cumorah

IN CHAPTER 1 we stated that Mesoamerica was the most probable location for the Book of Mormon setting. If that's the case, as most Latter-day Saint archaeologists theorize, then how do we account for the Hill Cumorah being in the state of New York? Is the hill named Cumorah in New York the same hill where both the Nephites and the Jaredites met their demise? Ether 15:11 and Mormon 6:4–6 tell us that the Nephite Cumorah and the Jaredite Ramah are the same hill.

The Hill Cumorah was located not many days' journey from the narrow neck of land. The New York Hill Cumorah is not. Cumorah was surrounded by cities. The New York Hill Cumorah was not. The Hill Cumorah was close to the borders of an eastern sea. The Hill Cumorah in New York does not meet any of these geographical features as spelled out in the Book of Mormon. Many Latter-day Saint archaeologists and scholars think the Hill Cumorah of the Book of Mormon may be located in Veracruz, Mexico. For one view and analysis of this subject, see David Palmer's book, *In Search of Cumorah.*[85]

Mormon, the father of Moroni, wrote that he put the records of the Nephite people in the Hill Cumorah (see Mormon 6:6) and gave the abridged plates that are called the Book of Mormon to his son Moroni. However, Moroni never said where he buried the plates his father gave him (see Mormon 8:14).

The Nephite nation ended in approximately AD 385 (see Mormon 6:15–22). After Mormon was killed, his son Moroni wrote: "And I even remain alone to write the sad tale of the destruction of my people. . . . Therefore I will write and hide up the records in the earth; and whither I go it mattereth not" (Mormon 8:3–4). Following this great disaster, Moroni had approximately thirty-five years to travel and deposit the plates where the Lord directed him to go. Moroni closed his record around AD 421 (see Moroni 10:1).

Where did Moroni travel from, and where did he go? There are two interesting hand-drawn maps viewed by H. Donl Peterson, who located them in the Church archives. Dr. Peterson was a professor of ancient scripture at Brigham Young University before his death. His findings on these maps are reported in a volume of the Book of Mormon Symposium Series.[86] The two maps were apparently drawn by the same hand, as they are very similar. Patriarch William McBride, who was a contemporary of Joseph Smith, had possession of the maps. He claimed that Joseph Smith was their ultimate source.

The maps were entitled "A chart, and description of Moroni's travels through this country." Moroni's route is sketched from the land Bountiful in Central America, listed as the starting point, to the Hill Cumorah in New York state. Many stops are shown along the way. These maps make it clear that the last battles between the Nephites and Lamanites were in Mesoamerica, where Moroni started his long journey.

There is no official statement as to the geography of the Book of Mormon, nor is there revelation from the General Authorities as to whether the Hill Cumorah in New York is the place where the Nephites had their last battle, or even if there is an original Cumorah in Mesoamerica. After all, there were two Bountifuls mentioned in the Book of Mormon—one in the promised land (America) and one in the Near East, where Lehi's people lived before their sea voyage. Having one location named after another was and still is common.

The hill in New York where Joseph Smith removed the golden plates was first called the Hill Cumorah by Oliver Cowdery.[87] Nineteenth-century Latter-day Saints continued to call the hill by that name, and apparently Joseph Smith did not correct the idea.[84] However, the Saints did not have the knowledge that we do today regarding the archaeology of the Americas.

The reader may have heard that when Oliver Cowdery and Joseph Smith went to the Hill Cumorah, a miraculous event occurred. The hill opened and they walked into a cave that contained a large room. It was as light as day, rather than dark as a cave would be. Oliver and Joseph saw many piles of plates stacked as much as two feet high around the room. This story did not originate from the mouth of Joseph as far as we know. Brigham Young said the story came from other people who were familiar with it (see Journal of Discourses 19:38).[88]

Heber C. Kimball talked of this event and spoke of the vision that Joseph and others had when they went into a cave at Cumorah (see Journal of Discourses 4:105). When righteous individuals have visions, they can be taken anywhere in the world, or even to the heavens for that matter. Visions are not tangible; they are seen through spiritual eyes.

To strengthen our point, the Hill Cumorah in New York is a drumlin, which was formed by the gravel and boulders deposited from a glacier. Such deposits by glaciers do not have caves.[89] The vision was most likely the original Hill Cumorah in Mesoamerica. Since the account is not directly from Joseph Smith, the details cannot be verified.

Nevertheless, many Latter-day Saints still lean toward the Hill Cumorah in New York being the one and only Hill Cumorah. Most Latter-day Saint archaeologists and scholars promote the Two-Cumorah Theory. We may not know for sure until the question is answered and revealed by the prophet, seer, and revelator of the Church.

Let us move on to subjects for which Joseph Smith was greatly ridiculed. These are the metal plates and the stone box where the engraved plates were deposited. Neither metal plates nor stone boxes had been found from the ancient world in the nineteenth century. Then the tables turned in the twentieth century. More recent discoveries have shown that metal plates were used to record accounts by ancient scribes and that many of these plates were stored in stone boxes.

INSCRIBED METAL PLATES

In the Old World, Hebrews were known to engrave some of their records on thin metal. One of the more notable examples is that of two copper scrolls discovered among the Dead Sea Scrolls. They date to the second century BC.[90] These metal scrolls were hidden and preserved in caves when the Jewish communities were dying out. Having survived for more than two thousand years, the scrolls were discovered in 1952. The Dead Sea Scrolls have now been translated by scholars, with most of the text published and available to the public.

But what about the inscribed metal plates that Joseph Smith claimed composed the Book of Mormon? In the last eighty years it has been discovered that people in many Old World cultures used metal plates. The history of the vast number of plates inscribed anciently cannot be covered in this writing, but some of the more important ones are listed below.

- Small gold plate, Djokha Umma, Mesopotamia, modern Iraq (2450 BC) (Louvre, Paris, France)

- Gold wafer, "Tablet of Shalmaneser III" (859–825 BC) from Kalat Shergat, Mesopotamia, modern Iraq (Oriental Institute, University of Chicago Museum)

- Gold and silver plates of Darius I, Persepolis, Iran (518–515 BC) (National Archaeological Museum, Tehran, Iran) (see Fig. 67)

- Gold Plates, Pyrgi, Italy (500 BC) (National Museum of Villa Guilia, Rome)[88]

Figure 67. The plates of King Daruis, Persepolis, Iran.[87]

The Jaredites, the earliest civilization chronicled in the Book of Mormon, left records on gold plates for future generations (see Mosiah 8:9; Ether 1:4). Since the Jaredites came from Mesopotamia at the time of the Tower of Babel, the discovery of gold plates from this early period in the Old World would be significant. According to Richard Ellis, a Near Eastern specialist, inscriptions on various types of metallic plates go back to as early as 2700–2500 BC in Mesopotamia.[91] Inscribing gold plates was not unique to the Jaredite people; contemporaries in their homeland inscribed metal plates as well.

Isaiah was commanded to engrave prophecy on brass, and even in the time of Moses the Israelites used a kind of brass that was an alloy of copper and gold.[17] It is therefore no surprise that the brass plates were kept by Laban at his house in Jerusalem. Since these plates covered the scriptures and genealogies of the Hebrew people up to that time, it was important to the Lord that Nephi obtain these records to take with his people on their trip to the promised land in the New World.

There has also been much controversy about the Book of Mormon plates being composed of gold. If they were of solid gold, they would have weighed too much even for the mighty Moroni to take with him on his travels. However, it is believed by many scholars that the plates were not solid gold but "had the appearance of gold," as Joseph Smith stated.[92] This indicates that the plates were a combination of gold and another metal.

A metal composite called tumbaga by the Spanish was used in ancient Mesoamerica. It has been suggested by Latter-day Saint scholars that tumbaga was the composition of the plates of the Book of Mormon. Read H. Putnam tells us about tumbaga in an article in the *Improvement Era*:

> Tumbaga is an alloy of gold and copper, the only two colored metals known to man. . . . Tumbaga, the magic metal, can be cast, drawn, hammered, gilded, soldered, welded, plated, hardened, annealed, polished, engraved, embossed, and inlaid. . . . We must conclude that ancient American smiths had sufficient knowledge and skill to make a set of plates using the alloy that the Spaniards called tumbaga. The plates of the Book of Mormon, we allege, were of this alloy and were probably of between 8- and 12-carat gold. They thus appear to have weighed between 53 and 86 pounds.[93]

The Nephites most likely used tumbaga, which can be polished and engraved. Since the Nephites wrote in a script that no one else understood (see Mormon 9:34), it is reasonable that no other plates of this type would be found in Mesoamerica. The library of the Nephites still remains in the Hill Cumorah and will be revealed at the Lord's choosing.

However, there are a few examples of hammered metal objects in Mesoamerica that we can look to for an example. At Chichen Itza on the Yucatan Peninsula, Mexico, there exists a large natural well called a *cenote*. In ancient times, thin, embossed gold discs were thrown into the cenote as a sacred offering (see Fig. 68). Most of the disks have illustrations, but one has a Maya inscription.[90] Note the victorious warrior on Figure 68. He has a long beard, as do many other men on gold disks from Chichen Itza.

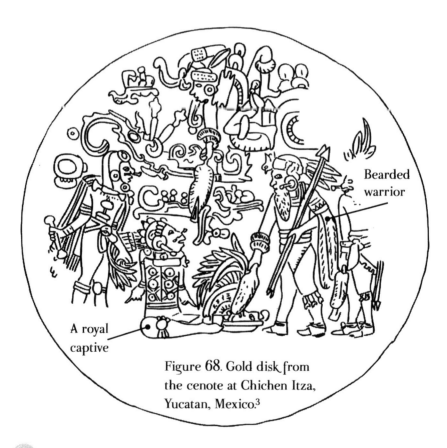

Bearded warrior

A royal captive

Figure 68. Gold disk from the cenote at Chichen Itza, Yucatan, Mexico.[3]

In a few legends, some Mesoamericans had books of gold, but they cannot be verified. Hyatt Verrill, an archaeologist who was not a Latter-day Saint, remarked about one of these legends that has a very "Book of Mormon feel" to it:

> According to tradition a complete history of the Maya was recorded in the Golden Book of the Mayas which, if it actually existed, as it probably did, was so carefully hidden to prevent it from falling into the hands of the Spaniards that it never has been found.[94]

There is another story worth mentioning, but again, we do not have the source where it originally came from or more evidence to support the argument. According to a nineteenth-century historian of the Mixtecs (a culture in ancient Mexico), they kept hieroglyphic records on thin gold plates.[22] The Mixtecs made several of the folded codices that we have today, so they definitely were record keepers.

STONE BOXES

Did you notice the Plates of Darius I in the list above of ancient plates and the associated illustration in Figure 67? The plates of Darius date to the time of Lehi. These inscribed plates of gold and silver were preserved in a stone box, similar to the Book of Mormon plates. Since the discovery of the Plates of Darius, other metal plates have been found in stone boxes as well.[90]

In Joseph Smith's time, no stone boxes had been found in Mesoamerica. Today, we know of many that have been discovered, further supporting the truth of his story. The stone boxes were for keeping and preserving sacred objects. In Mesoamerica, we show two illustrations of stone boxes (see Figs. 69 and 70 on page 100). One of these decorative boxes has the World Tree, and the other has a bearded man.

A variety of objects have been found in ancient American stone boxes, from jewelry and clothing to ritual tools, and in one case, an ancient record. Robert Wauchope, a famous archaeologist, describes a stone box found in the late nineteenth century.

> On her deathbed, Alice Le Plongeon (wife of [archaeologist] Augustus Le Plongeon) turned over to an intimate friend many of her husband's drawings and notes and evidently tried to

tell the location of another spectacular discovery they claimed to have made and covered again in 1875—some underground rooms containing stone boxes holding perfectly preserved ancient records of the Maya.[96]

The Lamanites were no doubt intermixed with many native Indians of the Americas, but did they keep records? There is a clue in Helaman 3:15, which reads: "But behold, there are many books and many records of every kind, and they have been kept *chiefly* by the Nephites."

The keyword in this scripture is *chiefly*. The word *chiefly* means primarily, mainly, essentially, mostly, predominantly, or largely. In other words, the Nephites inscribed most of the books, but another people also wrote books and records to a lesser degree than did the Nephites. We can assume that the connotations in this scripture could apply to the Lamanites, who mixed with other races in Mesoamerica.

Left: Figure 69. Stone box with bird and World Tree, Chalco, Mexico, Mexico.[17]

World Tree

Right: Figure 70. Stone box with bearded man wearing a Jaguar skin.[95]

We know from the scriptures that a man named Hagoth built ships. These ships were launched and took many people to unknown places northward (see Alma 63). We do not have a record of those who left for other parts of the Americas or even for islands in the Pacific (see 2 Nephi 10:21), but we do have the records that the Lord wanted us to have today through the Nephites (see 3 Nephi 23:4), which will bring us nearer to Jesus Christ than any other book.

CONCLUSION

The Book of Mormon is real, and so were the ancient people found within its pages who lived and breathed just as we do today. They believed that they were a chosen people (see Alma 31:28; Helaman 15:3) and that they were destined to find a promised land (see 1 Nephi 2:20). The Quiché Maya believed the same. Michel Graulich wrote: "The Quiché [Maya] claim to be a chosen people who are on their way to a land promised by their god."[50] The Quiché Maya could very well be a remnant of the Lamanites. They came from Tabasco, Mexico, and were influenced by ancient Mexican cultures.

The Book of Mormon does not include all the plates that Joseph Smith was directed to uncover in Palmyra, New York. Most of these plates were sealed and were not to be translated. 2 Nephi 27:10 reads:

> But the words which are sealed he shall not deliver, neither shall he deliver the book. For the book shall be sealed by the power of God, and the revelation which was sealed shall be kept in the book until the own due time of the Lord, that they may come forth; for behold, they reveal all things from the foundation of the world unto the end thereof.

The grand library still remains in the Hill Cumorah, and someday we hope to have available a translation of all the records, as we must hope that the reason the Nephites were commanded to make numerous plates and to record their history and gospel doctrine was so that one day the entire world would have these writings.

Below we have a list of items that were common to both the Book of Mormon peoples and those of Mesoamerica. If Joseph Smith wrote a fictional history, as his critics believe, how did he so accurately know the background, culture, skills, and beliefs of the people of ancient Mesoamerica? Until the twentieth century, archaeologists had a limited knowledge of these subjects and did not make these discoveries until after Joseph Smith's time. Every single item on the list below of things mentioned in the Book of Mormon was known to have been accomplished, or was a belief system, to the ancient people of Mesoamerica.

We make a short list of scriptures for each item. Some of the scriptures from 1 Nephi happened before Lehi's group came to the New World. However, these scriptures are important because they speak of inherited skills or beliefs that were carried on through the following generations when Lehi's people came to the land of promise in the Americas.

TRADITIONS

Kept old laws of their religion (2 Nephi 5:10)
Genealogy was important (Omni 1)
Kings and royalty (1 Nephi 9:4)
Kept records (2 Nephi 5:33)

SKILLS

Writing (1 Nephi 1:2)
Cement (Helaman 3:7)
Metallurgy and metal plates (1 Nephi 19:1)
Seafaring vessels (1 Nephi 17:19)
Built temples (2 Nephi 5:16)
Large stone engravings (Omni 20)

WAR

Numerous wars (Mormon 8:8)
Bows, arrows, swords, cimeters (scimitars), clubs, and slings (Mosiah 9:16)
Head-plates, breastplates, and shields (Alma 46:13)
Thick clothing for protection in war (Alma 43:19)
Binding enemies with strong cords (Alma 14:22)
Shedding blood for power (Alma 44:2)
Made prisoners slaves (Mosiah 7:15)
Fortifications around cities (Alma 48:8)
Held the enemy by the hair (1 Nephi 4:18)

Slaying kings in ceremony (Mosiah 19:23–24)
Human sacrifice (Mormon 4:14)
Cannibalism (Moroni 9:10)

RELIGION

Tree of Life (1 Nephi 8)
God descends from heaven (1 Nephi 11:7)
Knowledge of creation of earth (2 Nephi 1:10)
Knowledge of first parents in paradise (Alma 12:21–23)
Creation by word (Jacob 4:9)
Priestcraft (2 Nephi 26:29)
Sacrificial offerings made (Mosiah 2:3)
Fasting (Mosiah 27:22)
Mankind "must be born again" (Mosiah 27:25)
Life is endless (Mosiah 16:9)
Premortal state (Alma 13:3)
Baptism (2 Nephi 9:23; Moroni 8:9)
Resurrection (Alma 11:45)
Tree springing from man, indicating everlasting life (Alma 33:23)

MISCELLANEOUS BELIEFS

Going to a "land of promise" (1 Nephi 2:20)
Trees and branches symbolic of people (1 Nephi 10:12, 14)
Four quarters of the earth (1 Nephi 19:16)
Roads connecting cities (3 Nephi 6:8)
Duality—an opposition of all things (2 Nephi 2:11)
Seven tribes (Jacob 1:13)
Mother earth (2 Nephi 9:7)
Merchants and trade (3 Nephi 6:11)
Hot climate (Alma 51:33)
Knowledge of the Great Flood (Alma 10:22)

The plates that contained the Book of Mormon from the Hill Cumorah in New York are important to all Latter-day Saints. The promises of the Lord are both to the Gentiles and to the people of the Book of Mormon, specifically the Lamanites and their descendants. The Nephite prophets knew that their brethren, the Lamanites, would come to know of their fathers and the gospel of Christ in the future, as their fathers would "speak from the dust" through this sacred record (Enos 16–18; 2 Nephi 3:19).

The Gentiles mentioned in the Book of Mormon include today's Latter-day Saints. The Book of Mormon came to the descendants of the Indians through Joseph Smith and the Latter-day Saints. 3 Nephi 26:8 states:

> I [Mormon] have written them [the record on plates] to the intent that they may be brought again unto this people [people of the Book of Mormon], from the Gentiles, according to the words which Jesus hath spoken.

Over fifteen hundred years have passed since the close of the Book of Mormon in AD 421. We know from archaeological evidence that wars continued throughout the Americas from ancient times. The population of the Indians was always mobile, even before the Spanish Conquest. It is logical to assume that the seed of the Nephites, Lamanites, Mulekites, and Jaredites (mixed with other native peoples) spread out over both North and South America. Because there was a great apostasy among them, a time when they no longer followed gospel principles or took upon themselves the name of Jesus Christ, Latter-day Saints sometimes refer to the American Indians as Lamanites. Although it is true that not all American Indians are Lamanites, all of the remnants of the Lamanites are American Indians.

Today, the Lamanites are returning to the voice of their shepherd in enormous numbers and are enjoying the fruits of the gospel throughout the Americas. Remember, the American Indians are mixed in with the House of Israel through the Lamanites. Many of the Gentiles mentioned in the Book of Mormon also have the blood of Israel, because the Israelites were dispersed throughout the ancient world.

Gentiles, who are not literal descendants of Israel, are adopted in that lineage through Abraham when they accept the gospel. Abraham 2:10 explains this principle: "For as many as receive this Gospel shall be called after thy name [Abraham], and shall be accounted thy seed, and shall rise up and bless thee, as their father."

It is important that all who read the Book of Mormon take the following scripture seriously:

And I [Moroni] exhort you to remember these things; for the time speedily cometh that ye shall know that I lie not, for ye shall see me at the bar of God; and the Lord God will say unto you: Did I not declare my words unto you, which were written by this man, like as one crying from the dead, yea, even as one speaking out of the dust? (Moroni 10:27.)

APPENDIX

○○○○○○

IN RECENT YEARS, exciting developments have taken place in Mesoamerican archaeology. The one we will focus our attention on is a spectacular pre-Classic site called San Bartolo in northeastern Guatemala. This ancient city flourished during Book of Mormon times and, as we shall see, had mythical stories. Whether the city of San Bartolo was Nephite or Lamanite, one has to remember that most of the time in the Book of Mormon, the people were not righteous and were constantly called to repentance by their prophets. Apostasy was evident in their teachings, but a glimmer of truth remained.

Several key artifacts have been found at San Bartolo. The first would be the unexpected remains of murals—forty feet in length and dating to 150–100 BC—discovered in 2001. These murals have been acclaimed as art masterpieces. The site of Bonampak, Chiapas, Mexico, was the only other site with extensive murals, but it dates eight hundred years later than the San Bartolo murals. Therefore, the San Bartolo murals are extremely important to scholars because, to the scholars' way of thinking, it pushes back in time the cultural development of the Maya.

The second significant find at San Bartolo is a well-developed hieroglyphic text dating to 300–200 BC (see Fig. 71). It had previously been thought that text with this level of sophistication did not appear

Figure 71.
Hieroglyphs
from San
Bartolo (drawn
from photo-
graph).[102]

until around AD 300. Much later texts can be read with 95 percent accuracy. Scholars are working on deciphering the early San Bartolo text and are very excited about this discovery. They hope to someday translate it.

The third important item at San Bartolo is what the murals relate to us as a pictographic narrative. The mural illustrations depict the creation of the world and the life, death, and resurrection of the maize god. The story of the maize god is known, particularly from the *Popol Vuh*, but it is now apparent that this is the same maize god that was worshipped by the Olmec (see Fig. 72). The artistic portrayal is nearly identical. The Maya were aware of Olmec traditions and many times emulated them, just as the Nephites did with the Jaredites' traditions, good and bad.

The Olmec in Mesoamerica flourished from approximately 1500−450 BC, covering the same era as the Jaredites in the Book of Mormon. As previously mentioned, most Latter-day Saint scholars have concluded that the Olmec and their neighbors are the Jaredites. Could any of the Jaredite people have survived their devastating wars? Chapter 2 gave us several selected names of the Nephites and Lamanites, such as Korihor, Coriantumr, Morianton, Shiblon, and Corianton, which were derived from Jaredite names. Therefore, it is fairly evident that some Jaredites survived the demise of the Jaredite nation. In other words, not all the Jaredite people were destroyed. Both the Olmec, as termed by those who research Mesoamerica, and the Jaredite nation, as chronicled in the Book of Mormon, met their doom through extensive war.

Why are the murals significant to Latter-day Saints? Because shades of the gospel are seen in the *Popol Vuh* and in the murals at San Bartolo. The *Popol Vuh* speaks of a feathered serpent called *Gucumatz* or "Quetzal Bird Serpent," who had a hand in the creation of the earth. This deity was mentioned in chapter 8. The San Bartolo murals depict a long, plumed serpent that symbolizes breath and wind, as do the feathered serpents in Quetzalcoatl mythology. As already noted, Quetzalcoatl, the Feathered Serpent, was a basic symbol of wind and the breath of life.

Figure 72. The Maya maize god of San Bartolo (drawn from photograph).[101]

Striding atop the serpent is the maize god, his wife, and attendants. In this case, because these figures are walking on the serpent's back, the Feathered Serpent is not just a support for them but also a path of sorts, the vehicle in which they chose to travel on their journey.

The serpent emerges from a flowering mountain known as Precious Mountain Place, which is of mythical origin. It represents life, fertility, and abundance. This mountain was considered to be in the center of the world, where the Tree of Life grew. This Flower Mountain was the place of ascent and resurrection.[101]

To the left of the scene is a gourd, representing a mother's womb, spewing five babies with umbilical cords. One baby is at the center (partially dressed), while the other four represent the four quarters of the world. Perhaps this scene represents the peopling of the earth.

After the North Wall at San Bartolo was discovered (discussed above), the West Wall was found. Illustrations of a center World Tree (Tree of Life) and four trees representing the cardinal points amid sacrifices representing water, land, sky, and paradise decorate the walls. The sacrifices were performed by the maize god. A great bird, repeated several times and symbolic of the high god, oversees the placement of trees and sacrifices. In this mural there is also a king in the guise of the maize god ascending to the throne. Maya kings would reenact their accession and the creation of their high god, who was king in the supernatural realm, or the heavens.[102]

The final section of this wall traces the maize god from his birth, through his life as ruler, through death, and finally into resurrection. This scenario brings order and fertility to the world.

The discovery of San Bartolo is causing a more thorough investigation of the pre-Classic period in Mesoamerica. We do not know what the implications of the San Bartolo murals and inscriptions will have in the future for Latter-day Saints, but each new discovery makes our understanding of the people of Mesoamerica clearer and, for Latter-day Saints, presents a possible reconstruction of religious thinking of the people in the Book of Mormon. Keep in mind, of course, that during the greater part of their history, they were not following gospel principles. It was their prophets who remained steadfast and righteous.

Scholars are working on decoding the earliest known Maya hieroglyphic text found at San Bartolo, which dates to approximately 250 BC. The glyphs are proving to be more complicated and thus more difficult to translate than those found dating five hundred years later. Not too many years ago, the date of 250 BC was absolutely unheard of for a Mayan text to have existed. The one glyph archaeologists have decoded is *ajaw*, meaning "lord," used as part of the title and names of kings. Because the text at San Bartolo is a full-blown developed script, scholars are sure that literacy must have developed much earlier than that time.

There are more than one hundred structures at San Bartolo, and the ongoing investigations prove to be very promising.

BOOKS AND SOURCES

〜〜〜〜〜

1   *Times and Seasons* 3:23. October 1, 1842.

2   Sorenson, John L. "Fortifications in the Book of Mormon
    Account Compared with Mesoamerican Fortifications,"
    in *Warfare in the Book of Mormon*. Salt Lake City: Deseret
    Book; and Provo: Foundation for Ancient Research and
    Mormon Studies, 1990.

3   Schele, Linda and David Freidel. *A Forest of Kings: The
    Untold Story of the Ancient Maya*. New York: William
    Morrow and Company, Inc., 1990.

4   Ruz, Mario Huberto. "Maya Daily Labors: A History in
    Lower Case," in *Maya*. New York: Rizzoli International
    Publications, Inc., 1998.

5   Coe, Michael D. and Mark Van Stone. *Reading The Maya
    Glyphs*. New York: Thames and Hudson, 2001.

6   Jones, Carl Hugh. "The 'Anthon Transcript' and Two
    Mesoamerican Cylinder Seals," in *Newsletter and
    Proceedings of the SEHA* 122. Provo, Utah: Society for
    Early Historic Archaeology, Sept 1970.

7   Sperry, Sidney B. "Were There Two Cumorahs?" in
    Journal of Book of Mormon Studies 4:1. Provo, Utah:
    Foundation for Ancient Research and Mormon Studies,
    spring 1995.

8   Sorenson, John L. *Nephite Culture and Society*. Salt Lake City: New Sage Books, 1997.

9   Ivins, Anthony W. "Are the Jaredites an Extinct People?" in *Improvement Era*. November 1902.

10   Yorgason, Blaine M., Bruce E. Warren, and Harold Brown, *New Evidences of Christ in Ancient America*. Arlington, Virginia: Stratford Books, and Book of Mormon Research Foundation, 1999.

11   Coe, Michael D. *America's First Civilization*. New York: American Heritage, 1968.

12   Wirth, Diane E. *Parallels: Mesoamerican and Ancient Middle Eastern Traditions*. St. George, Utah: Stonecliff Publishing, 2003.

13   Wuthenau, Alexander Von. *The Art of Terracotta Pottery in Pre-Columbian Central and South America*. New York: Crown Publishers, 1965.

14   Tate, Carolyn E. *Yaxchilan: The Design of a Maya Ceremonial City*. Austin: University of Texas Press, 1992.

15   Wuthenau, Alexander Von. *Unexpected Faces in Ancient America*. New York: Crown Publishers, 1975.

16   de Sahagun, Bernardino. *Historia General de las Cosas de Nueva Espana*, Introduccion al Primer Libro, Vol. II. Mexico: Editorial Nueva Espana, 1946. Cited in Diane E. Wirth, *Discoveries of the Truth*. California, 1978.

17   Wirth, Diane E. *A Challenge to the Critics: Scholarly Evidences of the Book of Mormon*. Bountiful, Utah: Horizon Publishers, 1986.

18   Kirchhoff, Paul, O. Guemes, and L. Reyes Garcia, eds. *Historia Tolteca-Chichimeca*. Mexico: INAH/CISINAH, 1976.

19   Tvedtnes, John. *The Most Correct Book*. Salt Lake City: Cornerstone Publishing, 1999.

20   Nibley, Hugh. "The Book of Mormon as a Mirror of the East," in the *Improvement Era*, 51. Salt Lake City: The Church of Jesus Christ of Latter-day Saints, 1948.

21   Deutsch, Robert. "New Bullae Reveal Egyptian-Style Emblems on Judah's Royal Seals," in *Biblical Archaeology Review* 28/4. July/August, 2002.

22   Sorenson, John L. *An Ancient American Setting for the Book of Mormon*. Salt Lake City: Deseret Book, and Provo, Utah: Foundation for Ancient Research and Mormon Studies, 1985.

23   Wilkinson, Richard H. *Reading Egyptian Art: A Hieroglyphic Guide to Ancient Egyptian Painting and Sculpture*. New York: Thames and Hudson, 1992.

24   Tvedtnes, John. "King Benjamin and the Feast of Tabernacles," in *By Study and Also by Faith*, vol. 2. Salt Lake City: Deseret Book, and Provo, Utah: Foundation for Ancient Research and Mormon Studies, 1990.

25   Schuster, Angela M. H. "Rituals of the Modern Maya," in *Archaeology* 50:4 (July/August 1997).

26   Thompson, J. Eric S. *Maya History and Religion*. Norman: University of Oklahoma Press, 1970.

27   Love, Bruce. "Yucatec Sacred Breads Through Time," in *Word and Image in Maya Culture: Explorations in Language, Writing, and Representations*. William F. Hanks and Don S. Rice, eds. Salt Lake City: University of Utah Press, 1989.

28   Hagen, Victor W. Von. *The Ancient Sun Kingdoms of the Americas*. Cleveland, Ohio: World Publishing Co., 1961. Cited in Diane E. Wirth, *Discoveries of the Truth*. California, 1978.

29   Clark, James R., ed. *Messages of the First Presidency*, vol. 4. Salt Lake City: Bookcraft, 1965.

30   Christenson, Allen J. *Popol Vuh: The Sacred Book of the Maya*. New York: O Books, 2003.

31   Freidel, David, Linda Schele, and Joy Parker. *Maya Cosmos: Three Thousand Years on the Shaman's Path*. New York: William Morrow & Company, Inc., 1993.

32   Leon-Portilla, Miguel. *Aztec Thought and Culture*. Norman: University of Oklahoma Press, 1963.

33   Seler, Eduard. *Codex Vaticanus B*, English Edition. Berlin and London: A. H. Keane, 1902–1903.

34   Norman, Garth V. Izapa Sculpture. Part 2: *Papers of the New World Archaeological Foundation, No. 30*. Provo: New World Archaeological Foundation, Brigham Young University, 1973.

35   Furst, Jill Leslie McKeever. *The Natural History of the Soul in Ancient Mexico.* New Haven: Yale University Press, 1955.

36   Nicholson, Henry B. "Religion in Prehispanic Central Mexico," in *Handbook of Middle American Indians* 10:1. Ed. by Robert Wauchope. Austin: University of Texas Press, 1971.

37   Brotherston, Gordon. *Image of the New World.* London: Thames and Hudson, 1979.

38   Hultkrantz, Ake. *The Religions of the American Indians.* Los Angeles: University of California Press, 1980.

39   Leon-Portilla, Miguel. "Introduction," in *Native Mesoamerican Spirituality.* New York: Paulist Press, 1980.

40   Brundage, Burr Cartwright. *The Phoenix of the Western World: Quetzalcoatl and the Sky Religion.* Norman: University of Oklahoma Press, 1981.

41   Fernandez, Adela. *Pre-Hispanic Gods of Mexico.* Mexico: Panorama Editorial, 1984.

42   Graulich, Michael. "Myth of Paradise Lost in Pre-Hispanic Central Mexico," in *Current Anthropology* 24:5. December 1983.

43   Keber, Eloise Quinones. *Codex Telleriano-Remensis: Ritual, Divination, and History in a Pictorial Aztec Manuscript.* Austin: University of Texas, 1995.

44   Merchant, W. W. ed. "Ode [Intimations of Immortality, from Recollections of Early Childhood]," *in Wordsworth Poetry and Prose.* Cambridge, Massachusetts: Harvard University Press, 1955.

45   Tozzer, A. M. *A Comparative Study of the Maya and the Lacandones.* New York, Archaeological Institute of America, The Macmillan Co., 1907.

46   Preuss, Mary H. *Gods of the Popol Vuh: Xmukane', K'ucumatz, Tojil, and Jurakan.* Culver City, California: Labyrinthos, 1988.

47   Bancroft, Hubert Howe. *The Native Races,* Vol. II. San Francisco: Bancroft & Co., 1883.

48   Thompson, J. Eric S. *Maya Hieroglyphic Writing,* Publication 589. Washington, D. C.: Carnegie Institution of Washington, 1950.

49   Pratt, Orson. *Journal of Discourses* 16. December 28, 1873.

50   Graulich, Michael. *Myths of Ancient Mexico*. Norman: University of Oklahoma Press, 1997.

51   Thompson, J. Eric S. *Mexico Before Cortez*. New York: Charles Scribners, 1937.

52   Barkay, Gabriel and Amos Kloner. "Jerusalem Tombs from the Days of the First Temple," in *Biblical Archaeology Review* 12/2. 1986.

53   Taylor, John. *The Government of God*. Liverpool, August 1852.

54   Gibson, Frances. *The Seafarers: Pre-Columbian Voyages to America*. Philadelphia: Dorrance & Co., 1974.

55   Ekholm, Gordon F. "Wheeled Toys in Mexico," in *American Antiquity* 11. 1946.

56   *Biblical Archaeology Review* 22:5. Sep/Oct 1996.

57   (Wheeled Animals): Boggs, Stanley H. "Salvadoran Varieties of Wheeled Figurines," in *Contributions to Mesoamerican Anthropology*, Pub. No. 1. Miami: Institute of Maya Studies of the Museum of Science, 1973; *Ancient Art of Veracruz*. Los Angeles: Ethnic Arts Council of Los Angeles, Los Angeles County Museum of Natural History, 1971; Stephan F. Borhegyi. "Wheels and Man," in *Archaeology* 23:1. January 1970; Thomas Stuart Ferguson. *One Fold and One Shepherd*. San Francisco: Books of California, 1958; Trude Dothan. "Philistine Fashion," in *Biblical Archaeology Review* 29:6. 2003.

58   Frankfort, Henri. *The Art and Architecture of the Ancient Orient*. Baltimore: Penguin Books, 1970.

59   Nicholson, H. H. *Topiltzin Quetzalcoatl: The Once and Future Lord of the Toltecs*. Boulder, Colorado: University Press of Colorado, 2001.

60   Leon-Portilla, Miguel. "Quetzalcoatl: espiritualismo del Mexico antiguo," in *Cuadernos Americanos* 105/4. 1959.

61   Carrasco, David. *Quetzalcoatl and the Irony of Empire: Myths and Prophecies in the Aztec Tradition*. Chicago: University of Chicago Press, 1982.

62   Stuart, George. "The Timeless Vision of Teotihuacan," in *National Geographic* 188:6. 1995.

63   Kaufmann, Carol. "Maya Masterwork," in *National Geographic*. December 2003.

64   Bierhorst, John. *The Mythology of Mexico and Central America*. New York: Morrow, 1990.

65   Nicholson, Irene. *Mexican and Central American Mythology*. New York: The Hamlyn Publishing Group, Ltd., 1967.

66   Gillette, Douglas. *The Shaman's Secret: The Lost Resurrection Teachings of the Ancient Maya*. New York: Bantam Books, 1977.

67   *Pearl of Great Price*. Joseph Smith—History.

68   de Cordova, Juan. *Arte en Lengua Zapoteca*. Mexico: 1578. Translated and cited in Tony Shearer. *Beneath the Moon and Under the Sun*. Albuquerque: Sun Publishing Company, 1975.

69   Tedlock, Dennis. *Popol Vuh: The Definitive Edition of the Mayan Book of the Dawn of Life and Glories of Gods and Kings*, revised edition. New York: Simon and Schuster, Inc., 1996.

70   Taube, Karl. *Aztec and Maya Myths*. Austin: University of Texas Press, 1993.

71   Cook, Roger. *The Tree of Life*. New York: Avon Books, a division of The Hearst Corporation, 1974.

72   Norman, V. Garth. "Stela 5," in *Book of Mormon Reference Companion*, gen. ed. Dennis L. Largey. Salt Lake City: Deseret Book, 2003.

73   Draper, Richard D. and Donald W. Perry. "Seven Promises to Those Who Overcome," in *The Temple in Time and Eternity*, eds. Donald W. Perry and Stephen D. Ricks. Provo, Utah: Foundation for Ancient Research and Mormon Studies, 1999.

74   Gray, John. *Near Eastern Mythology*. New York: Hamlyn Publishing, 1969.

75   Layard, Austen Henry. *The Monuments of Nineveh*. London, 1893.

76   Clark, John E. "A New Artistic Rendering of Izapa Stela 5: A Step toward Improved Interpretation," in *Journal of Book of Mormon Studies* 8:1. Provo, Utah: Foundation for Ancient Research and Mormon Studies, 1999.

77   Reilly, Kent. "Art, Ritual, and Rulership in the Olmec
      World," in *The Olmec World: Ritual and Rulership.*
      Princeton: The Art Museum, Princeton University, 1995.

78   Turner, Wilson G. *Maya Design.* New York: Dover, 1980.

79   Capitaine, Fernando Winfield. *La Estella 1 de la Mojarra.*
      Mexico: Universidad Nacional Autonoma de Mexico, 1990.

80   Reents-Budet, Dorie. *Painting the Maya Universe: Royal
      Ceramics of the Classic Period.* Durham: Duke University
      Press, 1994.

81   Parpola, Simo. "Monotheism in Ancient Assyria," in *One
      God or Many: Concepts of Divinity in the Ancient World*, ed.
      By Barbara Nevling Porter. Casco Bay Assyriological
      Institute, 2000.

82   Widengren, Geo. *The King and the Tree of Life in Ancient
      Near Eastern Religion.* Wiesbaden, Germany: Uppsala
      Universitets Arsskrift, 1951.

83   Tondrian, J. "Le tatouage sacre et la relig. de dionysiaque,"
      in *Aegyptus* 30. 1950.

84   Smith, William and Samuel Cheetham. *A Dictionary of
      Christian Antiquities* [reprint, 1987–80, London] vol. 2. New
      York: Kraus, 1968.

85   Palmer, David A. *In Search of Cumorah: New Evidences for
      the Book of Mormon from Ancient Mexico.* Bountiful, Utah:
      Horizon Publishers, 1981.

86   Peterson, H. Donl. "Moroni, the Last of the Nephite
      Prophets," in *The Book of Mormon Symposium Series: Fourth
      Nephi Through Moroni—From Zion to Destruction.* Provo,
      Utah: Brigham Young University Religious Studies Center,
      1988–1995.

87   Cowdery, Oliver. *Latter-day Saint's Messenger and Advocate.*
      July 1835.

88   *Journal of Book of Mormon Studies* 13:1–2. Provo, Utah:
      Foundation for Ancient Research and Mormon Studies,
      2004.

89   Tvedtnes, John A. Book Review on Brenton G. Yorgason,
      Little Known Evidences of the Book of Mormon. Salt Lake
      City: Covenant, 1989; In *Review of Books on the Book of*

Mormon 2. Provo: Foundation for Ancient Research and Mormon Studies, 1990.

90   Cheesman, Paul R. *Ancient Writing on Metal Plates.* Bountiful, Utah: Horizon Publishers, 1985.

91   Ellis, Richard S. "Foundation Deposits in Ancient Mesopotamia," in *Yale Near Eastern Researches* 2. New Haven and London: Yale University Press, 1968.

92   Smith, Joseph. *Times and Seasons* 3:9. March 1, 1842.

93   Putnam, Read H. "Were the Golden Plates made of Tumbaga?", in *The Improvement Era* 69:9. September 1966.

94   Verrill, Alpheus Hyatt and Ruth Verrill. *America's Ancient Civilizations.* New York: G. P. Putnam's Sons, 1953. Cited in Diane E. Wirth. *A Challenge to the Critics: Scholarly Evidences of the Book of Mormon.* Bountiful, Utah: Horizon Publishers, 1986.

95   Pasztory, Esther. *Aztec Art.* Norman: University of Oklahoma, 1998.

96   Wauchope, Robert. *Lost Tribes and Sunken Continents.* Chicago: University of Chicago Press, 1962. Cited in Diane E. Wirth. *A Challenge to the Critics: Scholarly Evidences of the Book of Mormon.* Bountiful, Utah: Horizon Publishers, 1986.

97   Aguilar, Manuel, et. al. "Constructing Mythic Space: The Significance of a Chiocomoztoc Complex at Acatzingo Viego, in *In the Maw of the Earth Monster.* James E. Brady and Keith M. Prufer, eds. Austin, Texas: University of Texas Press, 2005.

98   Sten, Maria. *The Mexican Codices and Their Extraordinary History.* Mexico D.F., 1974.

99   Nuttall, Zelia, ed. *The Codex Nuttall: A Picture Manuscript from Ancient Mexico.* New York: Dover Publications, Inc., 1975.

100   Diaz, Gisele and Alan Rodgers, with Introduction and Commentary by Bruce E. Byland. *The Codex Borgia: A Full-Color Restoration of the Ancient Mexican Manuscript.* New York: Dover Publications, 1993.

101   Saturno, William A., Karl A. Taube, David Stuart, and Heather Hurst. "The Murals of San Bartolo, El Peten,

Guatemala, Part 1: The North Wall," in *Ancient America*,
No. 7. Feb 2005.

102   "Final Intact Wall Mural Uncovered at San Bartolo," in
Institute of Maya Studies, Vol. 35, Issue 1. January 2006.

ABOUT THE AUTHOR

⊚⊚⊚⊚⊚

DIANE E. WIRTH received a BA in art from Brigham Young University and was a special post-graduate student at Harvard University. She has written several books, notably, *A Challenge to the Critics: Scholarly Evidences of the Book of Mormon* (Horizon Publishers, 1986) and *Parallels: Mesoamerican and Ancient Middle Eastern Traditions* (Stonecliff Publishing, 2003). Many of her articles have been published by the Foundation for Ancient Research and Mormon Studies at BYU and by *Ancient American* magazine.

A worldwide traveler, she has concentrated on the ancient sites in Mexico/Central America and the Middle East, and has studied their art, religion, and traditions.

Having lived in the states of Illinois, California, Colorado, Minnesota, and Massachusetts, she and her husband retired in St. George, Utah. They have two sons and five grandchildren. Sister Wirth has given over fifty presentations at LDS firesides and archaeological symposiums. Diane is also involved in genealogy and serves as a Family History Consultant.